Daniel G. Brinton

The Maya Chronicles

Daniel G. Brinton

The Maya Chronicles

ISBN/EAN: 9783743349889

Manufactured in Europe, USA, Canada, Australia, Japa

Cover: Foto ©ninafisch / pixelio.de

Manufactured and distributed by brebook publishing software (www.brebook.com)

Daniel G. Brinton

The Maya Chronicles

BRINTON'S LIBRARY OF
ABORIGINAL AMERICAN LITERATURE.
NUMBER I.

THE

MAYA CHRONICLES.

EDITED BY

DANIEL G. BRINTON, M.D.

D. G. BRINTON.
PHILADELPHIA.
1882.

PREFACE.

The belief that the only solid foundation for the accurate study of American ethnology and linguistics must be in the productions of the native mind in their original form has led me to the venturesome undertaking of which this is the first issue. The object of the proposed series of publications is to preserve permanently a number of rude specimens of literature composed by the members of various American tribes, and exhibiting their habits of thought, modes of expressions, intellectual range and æsthetic faculties.

Whether the literary and historical value of these monuments is little or great, they merit the careful attention of all who would weigh and measure the aboriginal mind, and estimate its capacities correctly.

The neglect of this field of study is largely owing to a deficiency of material for its pursuit. Genuine specimens of native literature are rare, and almost or quite inaccessible. They remain in manuscript in the hands of a few collectors, or, if printed, they are in forms not convenient to obtain,

as in the ponderous transactions of learned socie-
ties, or in privately printed works. My purpose
is to gather together from these sources a dozen
volumes of moderate size and reasonable price,
and thus to put the material within the reach of
American and European scholars.

Now that the first volume is ready, I see in it
much that can be improved upon in subsequent
issues. I must ask for it an indulgent criticism,
for the novelty of the undertaking and its inherent
difficulties have combined to make it less finished
and perfected than it should have been.

If the series meets with a moderate encouragement, it will be continued at the rate of two or
three volumes of varying size a year, and will, I
think, prove ultimately of considerable service to
the students of man in his simpler conditions of
life and thought, especially of American man.

CONTENTS.

INTRODUCTION.

THE CHRONICLES.

THE CHRONICLE OF CHAC XULUB CHEN.

I.

INTRODUCTION.

CONTENTS.

---

§ 1. *The Name "Maya."*

In his second voyage, Columbus heard vague rumors of a mainland westward from Jamaica and Cuba, at a distance of ten days' journey in a canoe.[1] Its inhabitants were said to be clothed, and the specimens of wax which were found among the Cubans must have been brought

---

[1] " Tambien diz [el Almirante] que supó que . . . aquella isla Española ó la otra isla Jamaye estaba cerca de tierra firme, diez jornadas de Canoa que podia ser sesenta á setenta leguas, y que era la gente vestida alli." Navarrete, *Viages*, Tom. I, pag. 127.

from there, as they themselves did not know how to prepare it.

During his fourth voyage (1503-4), when he was exploring the Gulf southwest from Cuba, he picked up a canoe laden with cotton clothing variously dyed. The natives in it gave him to understand that they were merchants, and came from a land called MAIA.[1]

This is the first mention in history of the territory now called Yucatan, and of the race of the Mayas; for although a province of similar name was found in the western extremity of the island of Cuba, the similarity was accidental, as the evidence is conclusive that no colony of the Mayas was found on the Antilles.[2]   These islands were

---

[1] "In questo loco pigliorono una Nave loro carica di mercantia et merce la quale dicevano veniva da una cierta provintia chiamata MAIAM vel Iuncatam con molte veste di bambasio de le quale ne erono il forcio di sede di diversi colori." *Informatione di Bartolomeo Colombo.*   It is thus printed in Harisse, *Bibliotheca Americana Vetustissima,* p. 473; but in the original MS. in the Magliabechian library the words "vel Iuncatam" are superscribed over the word "MAIAM," and do not belong to the text. (Note of Dr. C. H. Berendt.)   They are, doubtless, a later gloss, as the name "Yucatan" cannot be traced to any such early date. The mention of *silk* is, of course, a mistake.   Peter Martyr also mentions the name in his account of the fourth voyage : "Ex Guaassa insula et Taia Maiaque et cerabazano, regionibus Veraguæ occidentalibus scriptum reliquit Colonus, hujus inventi princeps," etc. *Decad.* III, Lib. IV.

[2] I have collected this evidence, drawing largely from the manu-

peopled by a wholly different stock, the remnants of whose language prove them to have been the northern outposts of the Arawacks of Guiana, and allied to the great Tupi-Guaranay stem of South America.

MAYA was the patrial name of the natives of Yucatan. It was the proper name of the northern portion of the peninsula. No single province bore it at the date of the Conquest, and probably it had been handed down as a generic term from the period, about a century before, when this whole district was united under one government.

The natives of all this region called themselves *Maya uinic*, Maya men, or *ah Mayaa*, those of Maya ; their language was *Maya than*, the Maya speech ; a native woman was *Maya ch̄uplal* ; and their ancient capital was *Maya pan*, the MAYA

script works on the Arawack language left by the Moravian missionary, the Rev. Theodore Schultz, and published it in a monograph, entitled : *The Arawack Language of Guiana in its Linguistic and Ethnological Relations.* (*Transactions of the American Philosophical Society*, 1871.) There was a province in Cuba named *Maiye;* see Nicolas Fort y Roldan, *Cuba Indigena*, pp. 112, 167 (Madrid, 1881). According to Fort, this meant "origin and beginning," in the ancient language of Cuba; but there is little doubt but that it presents the Arawack negative prefix *ma* (which happens to be the same in the Maya) and may be a form of *majùjun*, not wet, dry.

banner, for there of old was set up the standard of the nation, the elaborately worked banner of brilliant feathers, which, in peace and in war, marked the rallying point of the Confederacy.

We do not know where they drew the line from others speaking the same tongue.   That it excluded the powerful tribe of the Itzas, as a recent historian thinks,[1] seems to be refuted by the documents I bring forward in the present volume; that, on the other hand, it did not include the inhabitants of the southwestern coast appears to be indicated by the author of one of the oldest and most complete dictionaries of the language. Writing about 1580, when the traditions of descent were fresh, he draws a distinction between the *lengua de Maya* and the *lengua de Campeche*.[2] The latter was a dialect varying very slightly from pure Maya, and I take it, this manner of indicat-

---

[1] Eligio Ancona, *Historia de Yucatan*, Tom. I, p. 31 (Merida, 1878).

[2] *Diccionario Maya-Español del Convento de Motul.*   MS.   *Sub voce, ichech.*   The manuscript dictionaries which I use will be described in the last section of this Introduction.   The example given is :—

"Ichech ; tu eres, en lengua de Campeche ; *ichex*, vosotros seis ; *in en*, yo soy ; *in on*, nosotros somos.   De aqui sale en lengua de Maya, *tech cech ichech e*, tu que eres por ahi quien quiera," etc.

ing the distinction points to a former political separation.

The name Maya is also found in the form *Mayab*, and this is asserted by various Yucatecan scholars of the present generation, as Pio Perez, Crescencio Carrillo, and Eligio Ancona, to be the correct ancient form, while the other is but a Spanish corruption.[1]

But this will not bear examination. All the authorities, native as well as foreign, of the sixteenth century, write *Maya*. It is impossible to suppose that such laborious and earnest students as the author of the Dictionary of Motul, as the grammarian and lexicographer Gabriel de San Buenaventura, and as the educated natives whose writings I print in this volume, could all have fallen into such a capital blunder.[2]

The explanation I have to offer is just the re-

---

[1] See Eligio Ancona, *Hist. de Yucatan*, Tom. I, p. 37.

[2] "MAYA (accento en la primera); nombre proprio de esta tierra de Yucatan." *Diccionario de Motul*, MS. "Una provincia que llamavan de la *Maya*, de la qual la lengua de Yucatan se llama *Mayathan*." Diego de Landa, *Relacion de las Cosas de Yucatan*, p. 14. "Esta tierra de Yucatan, à quien los naturales llaman *Ma'ya*," Cogolludo, *Historia de Yucatan*, Lib. IV, Cap. III. "El antiguo Reyno de Maya ò Mayapan que hoy se llama Yucatan." Villagutierre, *Historia de el Itza y de el Lacandon*, p. 25. The numerous MSS. of the Books of Chilan Balam are also decisive on this point.

verse. The use of the terminal *b* in "Mayab" is probably a dialectic error, other examples of which can be quoted. Thus the writer of the Dictionary of Motul informs us that the form *maab* is sometimes used for the ordinary negative *ma*, no; but, he adds, it is a word of the lower classes, *es palabra de gente comun*. So I have little doubt but that *Mayab* is a vulgar form of the word, which may have gradually gained ground.

As at present used, the accent usually falls on the first syllable, *Ma'ya*, and the best old authorities affirm this as a rule; but it is a rule subject to exceptions, as at the end of a sentence and in certain dialects Dr. Berendt states that it is not infrequently heard as *Ma'ya'* or even *Maya'*.[1]

The meaning and derivation of the word have given rise to the usual number of nonsensical and far-fetched etymologies. The Greek, the Sanscrit, the ancient Coptic and the Hebrew have all been called in to interpret it. I shall refer to but a few of these profitless suggestions.

The Abbé Brasseur (de Bourbourg) quotes as the opinion of Don Ramon de Ordoñez, the author of a strange work on American archæ-

---

[1] *Nombres Geograficos en Lengua Maya*, folio, MS. in my collection.

ology, called *History of the Heaven and the Earth*, that *Maya* is but an abbreviation of the phrase *ma ay ha*, which, the Abbé adds, means word for word, *non adest aqua*, and was applied to the peninsula on account of the scarcity of water there.[1]

Unfortunately that phrase has no such, nor any, meaning in Maya; were it *ma yan haa*, it would have the sense he gives it; and further, as the Abbé himself remarked in a later work, it is not applicable to Yucatan, where, though rivers are scarce, wells and water abound. He therefore preferred to derive it from *ma* and *ha*, which he thought he could translate either "Mother of the Water," or "Arm of the Land!"[2]

The latest suggestion I have noticed is that of Eligio Ancona, who, claiming that *Mayab* is the correct form, and that this means "not numerous," thinks that it was applied to the first native settlers of the land, on account of the paucity of their numbers![3]

All this seems like learned trifling. The name may belong to that ancient dialect from which are derived many of the names of the days and

[1] Note to Landa, *Rel. de las Cosas de Yucatan*, p. 14.

[2] *Vocabulaire Maya-Francais-Espagnole, sub voce,* MAYA.

[3] *Hist. de Yucatan*, p. 37.

months in the native calendar, and which, as an esoteric language, was in use among the Maya priests, as was also one among the Aztecs of Mexico. Instances of this, in fact, are very common among the American aborigines, and no doubt many words were thus preserved which could not be analyzed to their radicals through the popular tongue.

Or, if it is essential to find a meaning, why not accept the obvious signification of the name? *Ma* is the negative "no," "not;" *ya* means rough, fatiguing, difficult, painful, dangerous. The compound *maya* is given in the Dictionary of Motul with the translations "not arduous nor severe; something easy and not difficult to do;" *cosa no grave ni recia; cosa facil y no dificultosa de hacer.* It was used adjectively as in the phrase, *maya u chapahal,* his sickness is not dangerous. So they might have spoken of the level and fertile land of Yucatan, abounding in fruit and game, that land to which we are told they delighted to give, as a favorite appellation, the term *u luumil ceh, u luumil cutz,* the land of the deer, the land of the wild turkey; of this land, I say, they might well have spoken as of one not fatiguing, not rough nor exhausting.

§ 2. *The Maya Linguistic Family.*

Whatever the primitive meaning and first application of the name Maya, it is now used to signify specifically the aborigines of Yucatan. In a more extended sense, in the expression "the Maya family," it is understood to embrace all tribes, wherever found, who speak related dialects presumably derived from the same ancient stock as the Maya proper.

Other names for this extended family have been suggested, as Maya-Kiche, Mam-Huastec, and the like, compounded of the names of two or more of the tribes of the group. But this does not appear to have much advantage over the simple expression I have given, though "Maya-Kiche" may be conveniently employed to prevent confusion.

These affiliated tribes are, according to the investigations of Dr. Carl Hermann Berendt, the following :—

1. The Maya proper, including the Lacandons.
2. The Chontals of Tabasco, on and near the coast west of the mouth of the Usumacinta.
3. The Tzendals, south of the Chontals.
4. The Zotzils, south of the Tzendals.
5. The Chaneabals, south of the Zotzils.

6. The Chols, on the upper Usumacinta.

7. The Chortis, near Copan.

8. The Kekchis, and

9. The Pocomchis, in Vera Paz.

10. The Pocomams.

11. The Mams.

12. The Kiches.   } In or bordering on

13. The Ixils.   Guatemala.

14. The Cakchiquels.

15. The Tzutuhils.

16. The Huastecs, on the Panuco river and its tributaries, in Mexico.

The languages of these do not differ more, in their extremes, than the French, Spanish, Italian and other tongues of the so-called Latin races; while a number resemble each other as closely as the Greek dialects of classic times.

What lends particular importance to the study of this group of languages is that it is that which was spoken by the race in several respects the most civilized of any found on the American continent. Copan, Uxmal and Palenque are names which at once evoke the most earnest interest in the mind of every one who has ever been attracted to the subject of the archæology of the New World. This race, moreover, possessed an abundant literature, preserved in written books, in characters which were in some degree phonetic. Enough of these remain to whet, though not to satisfy, the curiosity of the student.

The total number of Indians of pure blood speaking the Maya proper may be estimated as nearly or quite 200,000, most of them in the political limits of the department of Yucatan ; to these should be added nearly 100,000 of mixed blood, or of European descent, who use the tongue in daily life.[1] For it forms one of the rare examples of American languages possessing vitality enough not only to maintain its own ground, but actually to force itself on European settlers and supplant their native speech. It is no uncommon occurrence in Yucatan, says Dr. Berendt, to find whole families of pure white blood who do not know one word of Spanish, using the Maya exclusively. It has even intruded on literature, and one finds it interlarded in books published in Merida, very

[1] A discussion of the items of the census of 1862 may be found in the work of the Licentiate Apolinar Garcia y Garcia, *Historia de la Guerra de Castas de Yucatan*, Tomo I, Prologo, pp. lxvii, et seq. (Merida 1865.) The completion of this meritorious work was unfortunately prevented by the war. The author was born near Chan ꜫenote, Yucatan, in 1837, and was appointed *Juez de Letras* at Izamal in 1864.

much as lady novelists drop into French in their imaginative effusions.[1]

The number speaking the different dialects of the stock are roughly estimated at half a million, which is probably below the mark.

§ 3. *Origin of the Maya Tribes.*

The Mayas did not claim to be autochthones. Their legends referred to their arrival by the sea from the East, in remote times, under the leadership of Itzamna, their hero-god, and also to a less numerous immigration from the west, from Mexico, which was connected with the history of another hero-god, Kukul Càn.

The first of these appears to be wholly mythical, and but a repetition of the story found among so many American tribes, that their ancestors came from the distant Orient. I have elsewhere explained this to be but a solar or light myth.[2]

The second tradition deserves more attention from the historian, as it is supported by some of their chronicles and by the testimony of several

---

[1] See, for example, *El Toro de Sinkeuel, Leyenda Hipica* (Merida, 1856), a political satire, said to be directed against General Ampudia, by Manuel Garcia.

[2] D. G. Brinton, *The Myths of the New World ; a Treatise on the Symbolism and Mythology of the Red Race of America*, Chap. VI (2d Ed. New York, 1876).

of the most intelligent natives of the period of the conquest, which I present on a later page of this volume.

It cannot be denied that the Mayas, the Kiches and the Cakchiquels, in their most venerable traditions, claimed to have migrated from the north or west, from some part of the present country of Mexico.

These traditions receive additional importance from the presence on the shores of the Mexican Gulf, on the waters of the river Panuco, north of Vera Cruz, of a prominent branch of the Maya family, the *Huastecs*. The idea suggests itself that these were the rearguard of a great migration of the Maya family from the north toward the south.

Support is given to this by their dialect, which is most closely akin to that of the Tzendals of Tabasco, the nearest Maya race to the south of them, and also by very ancient traditions of the Aztecs.

It is noteworthy that these two partially civilized races, the Mayas and the Aztecs, though differing radically in language, had legends which claimed a community of origin in some indefinitely remote past. We find these on the Maya side narrated in the sacred book of the Kiches, the *Popol Vuh*, in the Cakchiquel *Records of Tecpan Atitlan*, and in various pure Maya sources which I bring forward in this volume.   The Aztec traditions refer to the Huastecs, and a brief analysis of them will not be out of place.

At a very remote period the Mexicans, under their leader Mecitl, from whom they took their name, arrived in boats at the mouth of the river Panuco, at the place called Panotlan, which name means "where one arrives by sea."   With them were the Olmecs under their leader Olmecatl, the Huastecs, under their leader Huastecatl, the Mixtecs and others.   They journeyed together and in friendship southward, down the coast, quite to the volcanoes of Guatemala, thence to Tamoanchan, which is described as the terrestial paradise, and afterwards, some of them at   least, northward and eastward, toward the shores of the Gulf.

On this journey the intoxicating beverage made from the maguey, called *octli* by the Aztecs, *cii* by the Mayas, and *pulque* by the Spaniards, was invented by a woman whose name was *Mayauel*, in which we can scarcely err in recognizing the national appellation *Maya.*[1] Furthermore, the invention is closely related to the history of the Huastecs. Their leader, alone of all the chieftains, drank to excess, and in his drunkenness threw aside his garments and displayed his nakedness. When he grew sober, fear and shame impelled him to collect all those who spoke his language, and leaving the other tribes, he returned to the neighborhood of Panuco and settled there permanently.[2]

The annals of the Aztecs contain frequent allusions to the Huastecs. The most important contest between the two nations took place in the reign of Montezuma the First (1440-1464). The attack was made by the Aztecs, for the alleged reason that the Huastecs had robbed and killed Aztec merchants on their way to the great fairs in Guatemala. The Huastecs are described as numerous, dwelling in walled towns, possessing quantities of maize, beans, feathers and precious stones, and painting their faces. They were sig-

---

[1] *Maya-uel* may be from *maya* and *ohel*, to know either intellectually or carnally; or the last syllable may be *uol*, will, desire, mind. This inventive woman would thus have been named "the Maya wit" (in the old meaning of the word).

[2] Sahagun, *Historia de la Nueva España*, Lib. X, Cap. XXIX, p. 12.

nally defeated by the troops of Montezuma, but not reduced to vassalage.[1]

At the time of the Conquest the province of the Huastecs was densely peopled; "none more so under the sun," remarks the Augustinian friar Nicolas de Witte, who visited it in 1543; but even then he found it almost deserted and covered with ruins, for, a few years previous, the Spaniards had acted towards its natives with customary treachery and cruelty. They had invited all the chiefs to a conference, had enticed them into a large wooden building, and then set fire to it and burned them alive. When this merciless act became known the Huastecs deserted their villages and scattered among the forests and mountains.[2]

These traditions go to show that the belief among the Aztecs was that the tribes of the Maya family came originally from the north or northeast, and were at some remote period closely connected with their own ancestors.

[1] Fray Diego Duran, *Historia de las Indias de Nueva España y Islas de Tierra Firme*, Cap. XIX (Ed. Mexico, 1867).

[2] See *Lettre de Fray Nicolas de Witt* (should be Witte), 1554, in Ternaux Compans, *Recueil des Pièces sur le Mexique*, p. 254, 286; also the report of the "Audiencia" held in Mexico in 1531, in Herrera, *Historia de las Indias Occidentales*, Dec. IV, Lib. IX, Cap. V.

§ 4. *Political Condition at the Time of the Conquest.*

When the Spaniards first explored the coasts of Yucatan they found the peninsula divided into a number of independent petty states. According to an authority followed by Herrera, these were eighteen in number. There is no complete list of their names, nor can we fix with certainty their boundaries. The following list gives their approximate position. On the west coast, beginning at the south—

1. *'Acalan*, on the Bahia de Terminos.
2. *Tixchel* (or Telchac?)
3. *Champoton* (Chakanputun, or Potonchan).
4. *Kinpech* (Campech or Campeche).
5. *Canul* (Acanul or H' Canul).
6. *Hocabaihumun.*
7. *Cehpech*, in which Merida was founded.
8. *Zipatan*, on the northwest coast.

On the east coast, beginning at the north—

9. *Choaca*, near Cape Cotoche.
10. *Ekab*, opposite the Island of Cozumel.
11. *Conil*, or of the Cupuls.
13. *Bakhalal*, or Bacalar.
14. *Chetemal.*
15. *Taitza*, the Peten district.

c

Central provinces—

16. *H' Chel* (or Ah Kin Chel) in which Itzamal was located.

17. *Zotuta*, of the Cocoms.

18. *Mani*, of the Xius.

19. *Cochuah* (or Cochva, or Cocolá), the principal town of which was Ichmul.

As No. 15, the Peten district, was not conquered by the Spaniards until 1697, it was doubtless not included in the list drawn up by Herrera's authority, so that the above would correspond with his statement.

Each of these provinces was ruled by a hereditary chief, who was called *batab*, or *batabil uinic* (*uinic*=man). He sometimes bore two names, the first being that of his mother, the second of his father, as *Can Ek*, in which *Can* was from the maternal, *Ek* from the paternal line. The surname (*kaba*) descended through the male. It was called *hach kaba*, the true name, or *hool kaba*, the head name. Much attention was paid to preserving the genealogy, and the word for "of noble birth" was *ah kaba*, "he who has a name."

Each village of a province was organized under a ruler, who was styled *halach uinic*, the true or real man. Frequently he was a junior member

of the reigning family. He was assisted by a
second in command, térmed *ah kulel,* as a lieutenant, and various subordinate officials, whose duties
will be explained in the notes to Nakuk Pech's
narrative.

Personal tenure of land did not exist. The town
lands were divided out annually among the members of the community, as their wants required,
the consumption of each adult being calculated at
twenty loads (of a man) of maize each year, this
being the staple food.[1]

§ 5. *Grammatical Observations.*

Compared with many American languages, the
Maya is simple in construction. It is analytic
rather than synthetic; most of its roots are mono-
syllables or dissyllables, and the order of their
arrangement is very similar to that in English. It
has been observed that foreigners, coming to

[1] I mention this particularly in order to correct a grave error in
Landa's *Relacion de las Cosas de Yucatan,* p. 130. He says,
"Suelen de costumbre sembrar para cada casado con su muger
medida de cccc piés que llaman *hun-uinic,* medida con vara de
XX pies, XX en ancho y XX en largo." The agrarian measure
uinic or *hun uinic* (one man) contained 20 *kaan,* each 24 yards
(*varas*) square. One *kaan* was estimated to yield two loads of
corn, and hence the calculation was forty loads of the staff of life
for each family. Landa's statement that a patch 20 feet square
was assigned to a family is absurd on the face of it.

Yucatan, ignorant of both Spanish and Maya, acquire a conversational knowledge of the latter more readily than of the former.[1]

An examination of the language explains this. Neither nouns nor adjectives undergo any change for gender, number or case. Before animate nouns the gender may be indicated by the prefixes *ah* and *ix*, equivalent to the English *he* and *she* in such expressions as *he-bear, she-bear.* The plural particle is *ob*, which can be suffixed to animate nouns, but is in fact the third person plural of the personal pronoun.

The conjugations of the verbs are four in number. All passives and neuters end in *l*, and also a certain number of active verbs ; these form the first conjugation, while the remaining three are of active verbs only. The time-forms of the verb are three, the present, the aorist, and the future. Taking the verb *nacal*, to ascend, these forms are *nacal, naci, nacac.* The present indicative is :—

[1] " La lengua castellana es mas difficultosa que la Maya para la gente adulta, que no la ha mamado con la leche, como lo ha enseñado la experiencia en los estranjeros de distintas naciones, y en los negros bozales que se han radicado en esta provincia, que mas facilmente han aprendido la Maya que la castellana." Apolinar Garcia y Garcia, *Historia de la Guerra de Castas en Yucatan.* Prologo, p. lxxv. (folio, Merida, 1865).

Nacal	in	cah,	I ascend.
Nacal	á	cah,	thou ascendest.
Nacal	ú	cah,	he ascends.
Nacal	c	cah,	we ascend.
Nacal	a	cah ex,	you ascend.
Nacal	u	cah ob,	they ascend.

When this form is analyzed, we discover that *in, á, ú, c, a-ex, u-ob,* are personal possessive pronouns, my, thy, his, our, your, their; and that *nacal* and *cah* are in fact verbal nouns standing in apposition. *Cah,* which is the sign of the present tense, means the doing, making, being occupied or busy at something. Hence *nacal in cah,* I ascend, is literally "the ascent, my being occupied with." The imperfect tense is merely the present with the additional verbal noun *cuchi* added, as—

Nacal in cah cuchi,	I was ascending.
Nacal á cah cuchi,	Thou wast ascending.
	etc.

Cuchi means carrying on, bearing along, and the imperfect may thus be rendered :—

"The ascent, my being occupied with, carrying on."

This is what has been called by Friedrich Müller the "possessive conjugation," the pronoun

used being not in the nominative but in the possessive form.

The aorist presents a different mode of forma-
tion :—

Nac-en, (i.e. Naci-en)	I ascended.
Nac-ech,	Thou ascended.
Naci,	He ascended.
Nac-on,	We ascended.
Nac-ex,	You ascended.
Nac-ob,	They ascended.

Here *en*, *ech*, *on*, *ex*, are apparently the
simple personal pronouns I, thou, we, you, and
are used predicatively. The future is also conjugated in this form by the use of the verbal *bin*,
binel, to go :

Bin nacac en,	I am going to ascend.
Bin nacac ech,	Thou art going to ascend.
	etc.

The present of all the active verbs uses this
predicative form, while their aorists and futures
employ possessive forms. Thus:—

Ten cambezic,	I teach him.
Tech cambezic,	Thou teaches him.
Lay cambezic,	He teaches him.

Here, however, I must note a difference of

opinion between eminent grammatical critics.
Friedrich Müller considers all such forms as—

Nac-en,   I ascended,

to exhibit "the predicative power of the true verb,"
basing his opinion on the analogy of such expressions as—

Ten batab en,   I (am) a chief.[1]

M. Lucien Adam, on the other hand, says:—
"The intransitive preterit *nac-en* may seem morpho-
logically the same as the Aryan *ás-mi*; but here
again, *nac* is a verbal noun, as is demonstrated by
the plural of the third person *nac-ob*, 'the ascenders.'
Nac-en comes to mean 'ascender [formerly] me.'"[2]

I am inclined to think that the French critic is
right, and that, in fact, there is no true verb in the
Maya, but merely verbal nouns, *nomina actionis*,
to which the pronouns stand either in the possessive or objective relations, or, more remotely, in
the possessive relation to another verbal noun in
apposition, as *cah, cuchi*, etc. The importance of
this point in estimating the structure of the language will be appreciated by those who have paid
any attention to the science of linguistics.

[1] Friedrich Müller, *Grundriss der Sprachwissenschaft*, II Band,
s. 309. (Wien, 1882).

[2] Lucien Adam, *Etudes sur six Langues Américaines*, p. 155.
(Paris, 1878).

The objective form of the conjugation is composed of the simple personal pronouns of both persons, together with the possessive of the agent and the particle *ci*, which conveys the accessory notion of present action towards. Thus, from *moc*, to tie :—

Ten c in moc ech,   I tie thee,

     literally,   I my present tying thee.

These refinements of analysis have, of course, nothing to do with the convenience of the language for practical purposes. As it has no dual, no inclusive and exclusive plurals, no articles nor substantive verb, no transitions, and few irregular verbs, its forms are quickly learned. It is not polysynthetic, at any rate, not more so than French, and its words undergo no such alteration by agglutination as in Aztec and Algonkin. Syncopated forms are indeed common, but to no greater extent than in colloquial English. The unit of the tongue remains the word, not the sentence, and we find no immeasurable words, expressing in themselves a whole paragraph, such as grammarians like to quote from the Eskimo, Aztec, Qquichua and other highly synthetic languages.

The position of words in a sentence is not dissimilar from that in English. The adjective precedes the noun it qualifies, and sentences usually follow the formula, subject—verbal—object. Thus :—

Hemac cu yacuntic Diose,   utz uinic.
He who loves God, [is] good man.
But transposition is allowable, as—

Taachili   u tzicic   u   yum   uinic.
Generally obeys his father, a man.

As shown in this last example, the genitive relation is indicated by the possessive pronoun, as it sometimes was in English, "John, his book ;" but the Maya is "his book John," *u huun Juan.*

Another method which is used for indicating the genitive and ablative relations is the termination *il.* This is called "the determinative ending," and denotes whose is the object named, or of what. It is occasionally varied to *al* and *el*, to correspond to the last preceding vowel, but this "vocalic echo" is not common in Maya. While it denotes use, it does not convey the idea of ownership. Thus, *u cħeen in yum*, my father's well, means the well that belongs to my father; but *cħenel in yum*, my father's well, means the well from which he obtains water, but in which he has no proprietorship. Material used is indicated by this ending, as *xanil na*, a house of straw (*xan*, straw, *na*, house).

Compound words are frequent, but except occasional syncope, the members of the compound undergo no change.   There is little resembling the incapsulation (*emboitement*) that one sees in most American languages.   Thus, midnight, *chumucakab*, is merely a union of *chumuc*, middle, and *akab*, night; dawn, *ahalcab*, is *ahal*, to awaken, *cab*, the world.

While from the above brief sketch it will be seen that the Maya is free from many of the difficulties which present themselves in most American tongues, it is by no means devoid of others.

In its *phonetics*, it possesses six elements which to the Spaniards were new.   They are represented by the signs:

ch, k, pp, th, tz, ɔ.

Of these the ch resembles dch, pronounced forcibly; the ɔ is as dz; the pp is a forcible double p; and in the th the two letters are to be pronounced separately and forcibly.   There remains the *k* which is the most difficult of all.   It is a sort of palato-guttural, the only one in the language, and its sound can only be acquired by long practice.

The *particles* are very numerous, and make up
the life of the language. By them are expressed
the relations of space and time, and all the finer
shades of meaning. Probably no one not to the
manor born could render correctly their full
force. Buenaventura, in his Grammar, enu-
merates sixteen different significations of the
particle *il*.[1]

The elliptical and obscure style adopted by most
native writers, partly from ignorance of the art of
composition, partly because they imitated the
mystery in expression affected by their priests,
forms a serious obstacle even to those fairly
acquainted with the current language. Moreover,
the older manuscripts contain both words and
forms unfamiliar to a cultivated Yucatecan of
to-day.

I must, however, not omit to contradict formally
an assertion made by the traveler Waldeck, and
often repeated, that the language has undergone
such extensive changes that what was written a
century ago is unintelligible to a native of to-day.
So far is this from the truth that, except for a few
obsolete words, the narrative of the Conquest,

[1] Gabriel de San Buenaventura, *Arte de la Lengua Maya*,
fol. 28 (Mexico, 1684).

written more than three hundred years ago, by the chief Pech, which I print in this volume, could be read without much difficulty by any educated native.

Again, as in all languages largely monosyllabic, there are many significations attached to one word, and these often widely different. Thus *kab* means, a hand; a handle; a branch; sap; an offence; while *cab* means the world; a country; strength; honey; a hive; sting of an insect; juice of a plant; and, in composition, promptness. It will be readily understood that cases will occur where the context leaves it doubtful which of these meanings is to be chosen.

These *homonyms* and *paronyms*, as they are called by grammarians, offer a fine field for sciolists in philology, wherein to discover analogies between the Maya and other tongues, and they have been vigorously culled out for that purpose. All such efforts are inconsistent with correct methods in linguistics. The folly of the procedure may be illustrated by comparing the English and the Maya. I suppose no one will pretend that these languages, at any rate in their present modern forms, are related. Yet the following are but a few of the many verbal similarities that could be pointed out:—

MAYA.	ENGLISH.
bateel,	battle.
chab,	to grab, to take.
hol,	hole.
hun,	one.
lum,	loam.
pol,	poll (head).
potum,	a pot.
pul,	to pull, carry.
tun,	stone.

So with the Latin we could find such similarities as *volah* = volo, *ɔa* = dare, etc.

In fact, no relationship of the Maya linguistic group to any other has been discovered. It contains a number of words borrowed from the Aztec (Nahuatl); and the latter in turn presents many undoubtedly borrowed from the Maya dialects. But this only goes to show that these two great families had long and close relations; and that we already know, from their history, traditions and geographical positions.

§ 6. *The Numeral System.*

The Mayas had a mathematical turn, and possessed a developed system of numeration. It counted by units and scores; in other words, it

was a vigesimal system.   The cardinal numbers
were :—

Hun,	one.
Ca,	two.
Ox,	three.
Can,	four.
Ho,	five.
Uac,	six.
Uuc,	seven.
Uaxac,	eight.
Bolon,	nine.
Lahun,	ten.
Buluc,	eleven.
Lahca,	twelve.
Oxlahun,	thirteen.
Canlahun,	fourteen.
Holhun,	fifteen.
Uaclahun,	sixteen.
Uuclahun,	seventeen.
Uaxaclahun,	eighteen.
Bolonlahun,	nineteen.
Hunkal,	twenty.

The composition of these numerals from twelve
to nineteen inclusive is easily seen. *Lahun* is
apparently a compound of *lah hun* (sc. *uinic*), "it
finishes one (man);" that is, in counting on the

fingers. *Lah* means the end, to end, and also the whole of anything. *Kal*, a score, is literally a fastening together, a shutting up, from the verb *kal*, to shut, to lock, to button up, etc.

From twenty upward, the scores are used :—

Hun tu kal,	one to the score, 21.
Ca tu kal,	two to the score, 22.
Ox tu kal,	three to the score, 23,

and so on up to

Ca kal,	two score, 40.

Above forty, three different methods can be used to continue the numeration.

1. We may continue the same employed between 20 and 40, thus :—

Hun tu cakal,	one to two score, 41.
Ca tu cakal,	two to two score, 42.
Ox tu cakal,	three to two score, 43,

and so on.

2. The numeral copulative *catac* can be used, with the numeral particle *tul* ; as :—

Cakal catac catul,	two score and two, 42.
Cakal catac oxtul,	two score and three, 43.

3. We may count upon the next score above, as:

Hun tu yoxkal,	one on the third score, 41.
Ca tu yoxkal,	two on the third score, 42.
Ox tu yoxkal,	three on the third score, 43.

The last mentioned system is that advanced by
Father Beltran, and is the only one formally
mentioned by him.   It has recently been carefully
analyzed by Prof. Leon de Rosny, who has shown
that it is a consistent vigesimal method.[1]

It might be asked, and the question is pertinent,
and is left unanswered by Prof. Leon de Rosny,
why *hun tu kal* means "one to the score," and
hun tu can kal is translated, "one on the fourth
score."   This important shade of meaning may be
given, I think, by the possessive *u* which originally
belonged in the phrase, but suffered elision.
Properly it should be,

Hun tu u can kal.

This seems apparent from other numbers where
it has not suffered elision, but merely incorpora-
tion, as :—

Hun tu yox kal＝hun tu u ox kal, 41.

Hu tu yokal＝hun tu u ho kal, 81.

This system of numeration, advanced by
Beltran, appears to have been adopted by all of
the later writers, who may have learned the Maya
largely from his Grammar.   Thus, in the transla-

---

[1] *Mémoire sur la numération dans la langue et dans l'Ecriture
sacrée des anciens Mayas*, in the Compte-Rendu of the Congrès
International des Américanistes, Vol. II, p. 439 (Paris, 1875).

tion of the Gospel of St. John, published by the
Baptist Bible Translation Society, chap. ii, v. 20;
Xupan uactuyoxkal hab utial u mental letile kulnaa,
"forty and six years was this temple in building;"[1]
and in that of the Gospel of St. Luke, said to have
been the work of Father Joaquin Ruz, the same
system is followed.[2]

Nevertheless, Beltran's method has been
severely criticised by Don Juan Pio Perez, who
ranks among the ablest Yucatecan linguists of
this century. He has pronounced it artificial, not
in accordance with either the past or present use
of the natives themselves, and built up out of an
effort to assimilate the Maya to the Latin numeral
system.

[1] *Leti u Ebanhelio Hezu Crizto hebix Huan*, London, 1869.
This translation was made by the Rev. A. Henderson and the
Rev. Richard Fletcher, missionaries to the British settlements at
Belize.

[2] *Letiu Cilich Evangelio Jesu Christo hebix San Lucas.* Londres,
1865. The first draught of this translation, in the handwriting of
Father Ruz, with numerous corrections by himself, is in the
library of the Canon Crescencio Carrillo at Mérida. A copy of it
was obtained by the Rev. John Kingdon of Belize, and printed in
London without any acknowledgment of its origin. It does not
appear to me to be accurate. For instance, chap. X, v. 1, "The
Lord appointed other seventy also," where the Maya has *xan
lahcatu cankal*, "seventy-two;" and again chap. XV, v. 4, the
ninety-nine sheep are increased to *bolon lahu uaxackal*, one
hundred and fifty-nine!

D

I give his words in the original, from his unpublished essay on Maya grammar.[1]

"Los Indios de Yucatan cuentan por veintenas, que llaman *kal* y en cierto modo tienen diez y nueve unidades hasta completar la primera veintena que es *hunkal* aunque en el curso de esta solo se encuentran once numeros simples, pues los nombres de los restantes se forman de los de la primera decena.

"Para contar de una à otra veintena los numeros fraccionarios ò las diez y nueve unidades, terminadas por la particula *tul* ò su sincopa *tu*,[2] se juntan antepuestas à la veintena espresada; por exemplo, *hunkal*, 20; *huntukal*, 21; *catukal*, 22; y *huntucakal*, 41; *catucakal*, 42; *oxtucankal*, 83; *cantuhokal*, 140, etc.

"El Padre Fr. Beltran de Santa Rosa, como puede verse en su *Arte de Lengua Maya*, formó un sistema distinto à este desde la 2ª veintena hasta la ultima, pues para espresar las unidades entre este y la 3ª veintena pone à esta terminandolas y por consiguiente rebajandole su valor por solo su anteposicion à dichas unidades fraccion-

[1] *Apuntes para una Gramatica Maya.* Por Don Juan Pio Perez, MSS. pp. 126, 128.

[2] "Me parece que *tu* es síncopa de *ti u*." (Note of Dr. Berendt.) There is no doubt but that Dr. Berendt is correct.

arias, y asi para espresar el numero 45 por ejemplo dice *ho tu yoxkal*, cuando *oxkal* ò *yoxkal* significa 60.

"No sé de donde tomó los fundamentos en que se apoya este sistema, quiza en el uso de su tiempo, que no ha llegado hasta este; aunque he visto en varios manuscritos antiguos, que los Indios de entonces como los de ahora, usaban el sistema que indico, y espresaban las unidades integras que numeraban, y para espresar el numero 65 dicen; *Oxkal catac hotul* ù *hotu oxkal*, que usa el Padre Beltran por 45.[1]

"Mas el metodo que explico esta apoyado en el uso y aun en el curso que se advierte en la 1ª y 2ª veintena é indican que asi deben continuar las decenas hasta la 20ª y no formar sistemas confusos que por ser mas ô menos análogos à la numeracion romana lo juzgaban mas ô menos perfectos, porque la consideraban como un tipo à que debia arreglarse cualquiera otra lengua, cuando en ellas todo lo que no este conforme con el uso recibido y corriente, es construir castillos en el aire y hacer reformas que por mas ingeniosas que sean, no pasan de inoficiosas."

In the face of this severe criticism of Father

---

[1] This is not correct. Beltran gives for 45, *hotu yoxkal*, which I analyze, *ho ti u u ox kal.*

Beltran's system, I cannot explain how it is that in Pio Perez's own Dictionary of the Maya, the numerals above 40 are given according to Beltran's system; and that this was not the work of the editors of that volume (which was published after his death), is shown by an autographic manuscript of his dictionary in my possession, written about 1846,[1] in which also the numerals appear in Beltran's form.

Three other manuscript dictionaries in my collection, all composed previous to 1690, affirm the system of Beltran, and I am therefore obliged to believe that it was authentic and current among the natives long before white scholars began to dress up their language in the ill-fitting garments of Aryan grammar.

Proceeding to higher numbers, it is interesting to note that they also proceed on the vigesimal system, although this has not heretofore been distinctly shown. The ancient computation was:

20 units	=one *kal*	=	20
20 kal	=one *bak*	=	400
20 bak	=one *pic*	=	8,000
20 pic	=one *calab*	=	160,000
20 calab	=one *kinchil* or *tzotzceh*	=	3,200,000
20 kinchil	=one *alau*	=	64,000,000

[1] *Apuntes del Diccionario de la Lengua Maya. Por un yucateco aficionado à la lengua*, 4to, pp. 486, MSS.

This ancient system was obscured by the Spaniards using the word *pic* to mean 1000 and *kinchil* to mean 1,000,000, instead of their original significations.

The meaning of *kal*, I have already explained to be a fastening together, a package, a bundle. *Bak*, as a verb, is to tie around and around with a network of cords; *pic* is the old word for the short petticoat worn by the women, which was occasionally used as a sac. If we remember that grains of corn or of cacao were what were generally employed as counters, then we may suppose these were measures of quantity. The word *kal* (*qal*), in Kiche means a score and also specifically 20 grains of cacao; *bak* in Cakchiquel means a corn-cob, and as a verb to shell an ear of corn, but I am not clear of any connection between this and the numeral. Other meanings of *bak* in Maya are "meat" and the *partes pudendas* of either sex.

Calab, seems to be an instrumental form from *cal*, to stuff, to fill full.[1] The word *calam* is used in the sense of excessive, overmuch. In Cakchiquel the phrase *mani hu cala*, not (merely) one

---

[1] "CAL: hartar ô emborrachar la fruta." *Diccionario Maya-Español del Convento de San Francisco*, Merida, MS. I have not found this word in other dictionaries within my reach.

cala, is synonymous with *mani hu chuvi*, not (merely) one bag or sack, both meaning a countless number.[1] In that dialect the specific meaning of *cala* is 20 loads of cacao beans.[2]

The term *tzotzcch* means deerskin, but for *kinchil* and *alau*, I have found no satisfactory derivation that does not strain the forms of the word too much. I would, however, suggest one possible connection of meaning.

In *kinchil*, we have the word *kin*, day; in *alau*, the word *u* month, and in the term for mathematical infinity, *hunhablat*, we find *hun haab*, one year, just as in the related expression, *hunhablazic*, which signifies that which lasts a whole year. If this suggestion is well grounded, then in these highest expressions of quantity (and I am inclined to think that originally *hun hablat*, one *hablat*=20 *alau*) we have applications of the three time periods, the day, the month, and the year, with the figurative sense that the increase of one over the other was as the relative lengths of these different periods.

---

[1] *Calepino en Lengua Cakchiquel por Fray* Francisco de Varea, MS. s. v. *chuvi*. This MS. is in the Library of the American Philosophical Society, Philadelphia.

[2] F. Pantaleon de Guzman, *Compendio de Nombres en Lengua Cakchiquel*, MS. This MS. is in my collection.

I think it worth while to go into these etymologies, as they may throw some light on the graphic representation of the numerals in the Maya hieroglyphics. It is quite likely that the figures chosen to represent the different higher units would resemble the objects which their names literally signify. The first nineteen‘ numerals were written by a combination of dots and lines, examples of which we find in abundance in the Codex Troano and other manuscripts. The following explanation of it is from the pen of a native writer in the last century:—

"Yantac thun yetel paiche tu pachob, he hunppel thune hunppel bin haabe, uaix cappele cappel bin haabe, uaix oxppel thuun, ua canppel thuune, canppel binbe, uaix oxppel thuun baixan; he paichee yan yokol xane, ua hunppel paichee, hoppel haab bin; ua cappel paichee lahunppiz bin; uaix hunppel paichee yan yokol xane, ua yan hunppel thuune uacppel bin be; uaix cappel thuune yan yokol paichee uucppel bin be; ua oxppel thuun yan yokole, uaxppel binbe; uaixcanppel thun yan yokole paichee (bolonppel binbe); yanix thun yokol (cappel) paichee buluc

piz; uaix cappel thune lahcapiz; ua oxppel thuun,
oxlahunpiz."

"They (our ancestors) used (for numerals in
their calendars) dots and lines back of them; one
dot for one year, two dots for two years, three
dots for three, four dots for four, and so on; in
addition to these they used a line; one line meant
five years, two lines ten years; if one line and
above it one dot, six years; if two dots above
the line, seven years; if three dots above, eight;
if four dots above the line, nine; a dot above
two lines, eleven; if two dots, twelve; if three dots,
thirteen."[1]

The plan of using the numerals in Maya differs
somewhat from that in English.

In the first place, they are rarely named without
the addition of a *numeral particle*, which is suffixed.
These particles indicate the character or class of
the objects which are, or are about to be, enumer-
ated. When they are uttered, the hearer at once
knows what kind of objects are to be spoken of.
Many of them can be traced to a meaning which

---

[1] *Codice Perez*, p. 92, MS. This is a series of extracts from
various ancient Maya manuscripts obtained by the late distinguished Yucatecan antiquary, Don Juan Pio Perez, and named
from him by Canon Crescencio Carrillo and other linguists. A
copy of it is in my collection. It is in quarto, pp. 258.

has a definite application to a class, and they have analogues in European tongues. Thus I may say "seven head of"—and the hearer knows that I am going to speak of cattle, or sheep, or cabbages, or similar objects usually counted by heads. So in Maya *ac* means a turtle or a turtle shell; hence it is used as a particle in counting canoes, houses, stools, vases, pits, caves, altars, and troughs, and some general appropriateness can be seen; but when it is applied also to cornfields, the analogy seems remote.

Of these numeral particles, not less than *seventy-six* are given by Beltran, in his Grammar, and he does not exhaust the list. Of these *piz* and *pel*, both of which mean, single, singly, are used in counting years, and will frequently recur in the annals I present in this volume.

By their aid another method of numeration was in vogue for counting time. For "eighty-one years," they did not say *hutuyokal haab*, but *can kal haab catac hunpel haab*, literally, "four score years and one year." The copulative *catac* is also used in adding a smaller number to a *bak*, or 400, as for 450, *hun bak catac lahuyoxkal*, "one *bak* and ten toward the third score." *Catac* is a compound of *ca tac, ca* meaning "then" or "and," and *tac*, which Dr. Berendt considered to be an irregular future of *talel*, to come, "then will come fifty," but which may be the imperative of *tac* (*tacah*, *tace*, third conjugation), which means to put something under another, as in the phrase *tac ex che yalan cum*, put you wood under the pot.

It will be seen that the latter method is by addition, the former by subtraction. Another variety of the latter is found in the annals. For instance, "ninety-nine years" is not expressed by *bolonlahutuyokal haab*, nor yet by *cankal haab catac bolonlahunpel haab*, but by *hunpel haab minan ti hokal haab*, "one single year lacking from five score years."

§ 7. *The Calendar.*

The system of computing time adopted by the Mayas is a subject too extensive to be treated here in detail, but it is indispensable, for the proper understanding of their annals, that the outlines of their chronological scheme be explained.

The year, *haab*, was intended to begin on the day of the transit of the sun by the zenith, and was counted from July 16th. It was divided into eighteen months, *u* (*u*, month, moon), of twenty days, *kin* (sun, day, time), each. The days were divided into groups of five, as follows:—

1. *Kan.*   6. *Muluc.*   11. *Ix.*   16. *Cauac.*
2. Chicchan.   7. Oc.   12. Men.   17. Ahau.
3. Cimi.   8. Chuen.   13. Cib.   18. Imix.
4. Manik.   9. Eb.   14. Caban.   19. Ik.
5. Lamat.   10. Ben.   15. Eɔnab.   20. Akbal.

The months, in their order, were:—

1. Pop.   7. Ɔe-yaxkin.   13. Mac.
2. Uo.   8. Mol.   14. Kankin.
3. Zip.   9. Chen.   15. Moan.
4. Zoɔ.   10. Yaax.   16. Pax.
5. Zeec.   11. Zac.   17. Kayab.
6. Xul.   12. Ceh.   18. Cumku.

As the Maya year was of 365 days, and as 18 months of 20 days each counted only 360 days, there were five days intervening between the last of the month Cumku and the first day of the following year. These were called "days without names," *xma kaba kin* (*xma*, without, *kaba*, names, *kin*, days), an expression not quite correct, as they were named in regular order, only they were not counted in any month.

It will be seen, by glancing at the list of days, that this arrangement brought at the beginning of each year, the days Kan, Muluc, Ix and Cauac in turn, and that no other days could begin the year. These days were therefore called *cuch haab*, "the bearers of the years" (*cuch*, to bear, carry, *haab*, year), and years were distinguished as "a year Kan," "a year Muluc," etc., as they began with one or another of these "year bearers."

But the calendar was not so simple as this. The days were not counted from one to twenty, and then beginning at one again, and so on, but by periods of 13 days each. Thus, in the first month, beginning with 1 Kan, the 14th day of that month begins a new "week," as it has been called, and is named 1 Caban. Twenty-eight of these weeks make 364 days, thus leaving one day to complete the year. When the number of these odd days amounted to 13, in other words when thirteen years had elapsed, this formed a period which was called "the *katun* of days," *kin katun*, and by Spanish writers an "indiction."

It will be readily observed by an inspection of the following table, that four of these indictions, in other words 52 years, will elapse before a "year bearer" of the same name and number recommences a year.

	1st year.	14th year.	27th year.	40th year
1	Kan	Muluc	Ix	Cauac
2	Muluc	Ix	Cauac	Kan
3	Ix	Cauac	Kan	Muluc
4	Cauac	Kan	Muluc	Ix
5	Kan	Muluc	Ix	Cauac
6	Muluc	Ix	Cauac	Kan
7	Ix	Cauac	Kan	Muluc
8	Cauac	Kan	Muluc	Ix
9	Kan	Muluc	Ix	Cauac
10	Muluc	Ix	Cauac	Kan
11	Ix	Cauac	Kan	Muluc
12	Cauac	Kan	Muluc	Ix
13	Kan	Muluc	Ix	Cauac.

A cycle of 52 years was thus obtained in a manner almost identical with that of the Aztecs, Tarascos and other nations.

But the Mayas took an important step in advance of all their contemporaries in arranging a much longer cycle.

This long cycle was an application of the vigesimal system to their reckoning of time. Twenty days were a month, *u* or *uinal;* twenty years was a cycle, *katun.* To ask one's age the question was put *haypel u katunil?* How many katuns have you? And the answer was, *hunpel katun,* one katun (twenty years), or, *hopel in katunil,* I am five katuns, or a hundred years old, as the case might be.

The division of the katuns was on the principle

of the Beltran system of numeration (see page 40), as,

xel u ca katun,   thirty years.

xel u yox katun,   fifty years.

Literally these expressions are, "dividing the second katun," "dividing the third katun," *xel* meaning to cut in pieces, to divide as with a knife. They may be compared to the German *dritthalb*, two and a half, or "the third a half."[1]

The Katun of 20 years was divided into five lesser divisions of 4 years each, called *tzuc*, a word with a signification something like the English "bunch," and which came to be used as a numeral particle in counting parts, divisions, paragraphs, reasons, groups of towns, etc.[2]

[1] All the examples in the above paragraph are from the Appendix to the *Diccionario Maya-Español del Convento de San Francisco, Merida*, MS. It also gives its positive authority to the length of the katuns, as follows : " Dicese que los Indios contaban los años à pares (*sic*), y cuando llegaba uno à veinte años, entonces decian que tenian *hunpel katun*, que son veinte años.' I think the words *à pares*, must be an error for *à veintenas* ; they may mean "in equal series."

[2] The *Diccionario de Motul* MS. has the following lengthy entries :—

" Tzuc : copete ô coleta de cabellos ; ô de crines de caballo, ô las barbas que echa el maiz por arriba estando en la mazorca ; y la cabeza que tienen algunas hachas y martillos en contra del tajo, y la cabeza del horcon, y las nubes levantadas en alto y que dan que denotan segun dice tempestad de agua. Partes, enpartimiéntos. Cuenta para pueblos, para partes, parrafos i articulos, diferencios y vocablos montones."

These *tzuc* were called by the Spaniards *lustros*, from the Latin *lustrum*, although that was a period of *five* years. Cogolludo says: "They counted their eras and ages, which they entered in their books, by periods of 20 years each, and by *lustros* of four years each. The first year they placed in the East [that is, on the Katun-wheel, and in the figures in their books], calling it *cuch haab;* the second in the West, called *Hijx;* the third in the South, *Cavac;* and the fourth, Muluc, in the North, and this served them for the Dominical letter. When five of the *lustros* had passed, that is 20 years, they called it a *Katun*, and they placed one carved stone upon another, cemented with lime and sand, in the walls of their temples, or in the houses of their priests."[1]

The historian is wrong in saying that the first year was called *cuchhaab;* that was the name applied to all the Dominical days, and as I have said, means "year bearer." The first year was called *Kan*, from the first day of its first month.

This is but one of many illustrations of how cautious we must be in accepting any statement of the early Spanish writers about the usages of the natives.

[1] *Historia de Yucatan*, Lib. IV, cap. v.

There is, however, some obscurity about the length of the *Katun*. All the older Spanish writers, without exception, and most of the native manuscripts, speak of it distinctly as a period of twenty years. Yet there are three manuscripts of high authority in the Maya which state that it embraced twenty-four years, although the last four were not reckoned. This theory was adopted and warmly advocated by Pio Perez, in his essay on the ancient chronology of Yucatan, and is also borne out by calculations which have been made on the hieroglyphic Codex Troano, by M. Delaporte, in France, and Professor Cyrus Thomas, in the United States.[1]

This discrepancy may arise from the custom of counting the katuns by two different systems, ground for which supposition is furnished by various manuscripts; but for purposes of chronology and ordinary life, it will be evident that the writers of the annals in the present volume adopted the Katun of twenty years' length; while on the other hand the native Pech, in his History of the Conquest, which is the last piece in the volume,

---

[1] M. Delaporte's calculations are mentioned by Leon de Rosny, *Essai sur le Déchiffrement de l'Ecriture Hiératique de l'Amérique Centrale*, p. 25 (Paris, 1876); Professor Thomas' will be found in the *American Naturalist*, for 1881, and in his *Study of the Codex Troano*, Washington, 1882.

gives for the beginning and the end of the Katun the years 1517–1541, and therefore must have had in mind one of twenty-four years' duration. The solution of these contradictions is not yet at hand.

This great cycle of $13 \times 20 = 260$ years was called an *ahau Katun* collectively, and each period in it bore the same name.

This name, *ahau Katun*, deserves careful analysis. *Ahau* is the ordinary word for chief, king, ruler. It is probably a compound of *ah*, which is the male prefix and sign of the *nomen agentis*, and *u*, collar, a collar of gold or other precious substance, distinguishing the chiefs. *Katun* has been variously analyzed. Don Pio Perez supposed it was a compound of *kat*, to ask, and *tun*, a stone, because at the close of these periods they set up the sculptured stone, which was afterwards referred to in order to fix the dates of occurrences.[1] This, however, would certainly require that *kat* be in the passive, *katal* or *kataan*, and would give *katantun*. Beltran in his Grammar treats the word as an adjective, meaning very long, perpetual.[2] But this is a later, secondary sense. Its usual signification is a body or batallion of war-

---

[1] Pio Perez, *Cronologia Antigua de Yucatan.* § VIII.

[2] " *Katun*, para siempre." Beltran de Santa Rosa, *Arte del Idioma Maya*, p. 177.

E

riors engaged in action.   As a verb, it is to fight,
to give battle, and thus seems related to the Cakchiquel *çat*, to cut, or wound, to make prisoner.[1]   The
series of years, ordered and arranged under a controlling day and date, were like a row of soldiers
commanded by a chief, and hence the name *ahau
katun*.

Each of these *ahaus* or chiefs of the Katuns was
represented in the native calendars by the picture
or portrait of a particular personage who in some
way was identified with the Katun, and his name
was given to it.   This has not been dwelt upon
nor even mentioned by previous writers on the
subject, but I have copies of various native manuscripts which illustrate it, and give the names of
each of the rulers of the Katuns.

[1] The following extracts from two manuscripts in my hands will
throw further light on this derivation —

KATUN: espacio de veinte años; *hun katun*, 20 años; *ca
katun*, 40 años, etc.

KATUN: batallon de gente, ordenada de guerra y ejercito asi, y
soldados cuando actualmente andan en la guerra.

KATUN (TAH, TÉ): guerrear, hacer guerra, ò dar guerra.

KATUNBEN: el que tiene tantas venteinas de años, segun el
numeral que se le junta, *hay katunben ech?* cuantas venteinas
de años tienes tu? *ca katunben en*, tengo dos venteinas.

DICCIONARIO DE MOTUL, MS., 1590.

ÇAT (he): generalmente sigᵃ cortar algo con acha, cuchillo ô
hiera; detener algo que se huya, atajarlo, etc.

Varea, *Calepino en Lengva Cakchiquel*, MS., 1699.

The thirteen *ahau katuns* were not numbered from 1 upward, but beginning at the 13th, by the alternate numbers, in the following order:—

13, 11, 9, 7, 5, 3, 1, 12, 10, 8, 6, 4, 2.

Various reasons have been assigned for this arrangement. It would be foreign to my purpose to discuss them here, and I shall merely quote the following, from a paper I wrote on the subject, printed in the *American Naturalist*, Sept., 1881:—

"Gallatin explained them as the numerical characters of the days "Ahau" following the first day of each year called Cauac; Dr. Valentini thinks they refer to the numbers of the various idols worshiped in the different Ahaus; Professor Thomas that they are the number of the year (in the indiction of 52 years) on which the Ahau begins. Each of these statements is true in itself, but each fails to show any practical use of the series; and of the last mentioned it is to be observed that the objection applies to it that at the commencement of an Ahau Katun the numbers would run 1, 12, 10, 8, etc., whereas we know positively that the numbers of the Ahaus began with 13 and continued 11, 9, 7, 5, etc.

"The explanation which I offer is that the number of the Ahau was taken from the last day Cauac preceding the Kan with which the first year of each Ahau began—for, as 24 is divisible by 4, the first year of each Ahau necessarily began with the day Kan. This number was the "ruling number" of the Ahau, and not for any mystical or ceremonial purpose, but for the practical one of at once and easily converting any year designated in the Ahau into its equivalent in the current

Kin Katun, or 52 year cycle. All that is necessary to do this is, to *add the number of the year in the Ahau to the number of the year Cauac corresponding to this "ruling number." When the sum exceeds 52, subtract that number.*

"Take an example: To what year in the Kin Katun does 10 Ahau XI (the 10th year of the 11th Ahau) correspond?

"On referring to a table, or, as the Mayas did, to a 'Katun wheel,' we find the 11th Cauac to be the 24th year of the cycle; add ten to this and we have 34 as the number of the year in the cycle to which 10 Ahau XI corresponds. The great simplicity and convenience of this will be evident without further discussion."

The important question remains, how closely, by these cycles, did the Mayas approximate to preserving the exact date of an event?

To answer this fairly, we should be sure that we have a perfectly authentic translation of their hieroglyphic annals. It is doubtful that we have. Those I present in this volume are the most perfect, so far as I know, but they certainly do not agree among themselves. Can their discrepancies be explained? I think they can in a measure (1) by the differing length of the katuns, (2) by the era assumed as the commencement of the reckoning.

It must be remembered that there was apparently no common era adopted by the Mayas; each province may have selected its own; and it is quite erroneous to condemn the annals off-hand for inaccuracy because they conflict between themselves.

§ 8. *Ancient Hieroglyphic Books.*

The Mayas were a literary people. They made frequent use of tablets, wrote many books, and covered the walls of their buildings with hieroglyphic signs, cut in the stones or painted upon the plaster.

The explanation of these signs is one of the leading problems in American archæology. It was supposed to have been solved when the manuscript of Bishop Landa's account of Yucatan was discovered, some twenty years ago, in Madrid. The Bishop gave what he called "an A, B, C," of the language, but which, when applied to the extant manuscripts and the mural inscriptions, proved entirely insufficient to decipher them.

The disappointment of the antiquaries was great, and by one of them, Dr. Felipe Valentini, Landa's alphabet has been denounced as "a Spanish fabrication."[1] But certainly any one acquainted with the history of the Latin alphabet, how it required the labor of thousands of years and the demands of three wholly different families of languages, to bring it to its perfection, should not have looked to find among the Mayas, or

[1] *Proceedings of the American Antiquarian Society,* 1880.

anywhere else, a parallel production of human intelligence. Moreover, rightly understood, Landa does not intimate anything of the kind. He distinctly states that what he gives are the sounds of the Spanish letters as they would be transcribed in Maya characters; not at all that they analyzed the sounds of their words and expressed the phonetic elements in these characters. On the contrary, he takes care to affirm that they could not do this, and gives an example in point.[1] Dr. Valentini, therefore, was attacking a windmill, and entirely misconstrued the Bishop's statements.

I shall not, in this connection, enter into a discussion of the nature of these hieroglyphics. It is enough for my purpose to say that they were recognized by the earliest Spanish explorers as quite different from those of Mexico, and as the only graphic system on the continent, so far as they knew it, which merited the name of writing.[2]

[1] The example he gives is the word *le*, which he says "para escrivirle con sus caracteres *habiendoles nosotros hecho entender que son dos letras, lo escrivian ellos con tres*," etc., thus plainly saying that they did not analyze the word to its phonetic radicals in their system. *Relacion de las Cosas de Yucatan*, p. 318.

[2] Las Casas says, with great positiveness, that they found in Yucatan "letreros de ciertos caracteres que en otra ninguna parte." *Historia Apologetica*, cap. CXXIII. I also add an interesting description of their books and letters, furnished by the companions of Father Alonso Ponce, the Pope's Commissary-Gen-

The word for book in Maya is *huun*, a mono-
syllable which reappears in the Kiche *vuh* and the
Huasteca *uuh*. In Maya this initial *h* is almost
silent and is occasionally dropped, as *yuunil Dios*,
the book of God (syncopated form of *u huunil
Dios*, the suffix *il* being the "determinative" ending). I am inclined to believe that *huun* is merely
a form of *uoohan*, something written, this being
the passive participle of *uooh*, to write, which, as
a noun, also means a character, a letter.[1]

eral, who traveled through Yucatan in 1586, when many natives
were still living who had been born before the Conquest (1541).
Father Ponce had traveled through Mexico, and, of course, had
learned about the Aztec picture-writing, which he distinctly con-
trasts with the writing of the Mayas. Of the latter he says : "Son
alabados de tres cosas entre todos los demas de la Nueva España,
la una de que en su antiguedad tenian caracteres y letras, con
que escribian sus historias y las ceremonias y orden de los sacri-
ficios de sus idolos y su calendario, en libros hechos de corteza
de cierto arbol, los cuales eran unas tiras muy largas de quarta ó
tercia en ancho, que se doblaban y recogian, y venia á queder á
manera de un libro encuardenada en cuartilla, poco mas, ó menos.
Estas letras y caracteres no las entendian, sino los sacerdotes de
los idolos, (que en aquella lengua se llaman 'ahkines'), y algun
indio principal. Despues las entendieron y supieron léer algunos
frailes nuestros y aun las escribien." (*Relacion Breve y Verdadera de Algunas Cosas de las Muchas que Sucedieron al Padre
Fray Alonso Ponce, Comisario-General en las Provincias de la
Nueva España*, page 392). I know no other author who makes
the interesting statement that these characters were actually used
by missionaries to impart instruction to the natives.

[1] "*uooh ;* caracter o letra.   *uooh* (tah, te) escribir.   *uoohan*,
cosa que esta escrita." *Diccionario de Motul*, MS.

Another name for their books, especially those containing the prophecies and forecasts of the priestly diviners, is said to have been *anahte;* or *analte.* This word is not to be found in any of the early dictionaries. The usual authority for it is Villagutierre Sotomayor, who describes these volumes as they were seen among the Itzas of Lake Peten, about 1690.[1]

These books consisted of one long sheet of a kind of paper made by macerating and beating together the leaves of the maguey, and afterwards sizing the surface with a durable white varnish. The sheet was folded like a screen, forming pages about 9 x 5 inches. Both sides were covered with figures and characters painted in various brilliant colors. On the outer pages boards were fastened, for protection, so that the completed volume had

[1] His words are : "Y satisfaciendoles por la quenta señalada, que ellos mismos tenian, de que vsavan, para ajustar sus antiguas Profezias, y los Tiempos de su cumplimiento, que eran vnos Caracteres y Figuras pintadas en vnas cortezas de Arboles, como de una quarta de largo cada hoja, ò tabilla, y del gruesso como de vn real de à ocho, dobladas à vna parte, y à otra, à manera de Viombo, que ellos llamavan Analtees," etc., *Historia de la Conquista de la Provincia de el Itza*, Lib. VII. cap I (Madrid, 1701). Pio Perez spells the word *anahté, Diccionario de la Lengua Maya*, s. v. following a MS. of the last century, given in the *Codice Perez*. The word *huunlté*, from *huunil*, the "determinative" form of "*hun*," and *té*, a termination to nouns which specifies or localizes them (e. g. *amay*, an angle, *amay té*, an angular figure, etc)., would offer a plausible derivation for *analté.*

the appearance of a bound book of large octavo size.

Instead of this paper, parchment was sometimes used. This was made from deerskins, thoroughly cured and also smoked, so that they should be less liable to the attacks of insects. A very durable substance was thus obtained, which would resist most agents of destruction, even in a tropical climate. Twenty-seven rolls of such parchment, covered with hieroglyphics, were among the articles burned by Bishop Landa, at Mani, in 1562, in a general destruction of everything which related to the ancient life of the nation. He himself says that he burned all that he could lay his hands upon, to the great distress of the natives.[1]

A very few escaped the destructive bigotry of the Spanish priests. So far as known these are.—

1. The Codex Tro, or Troano, in Madrid, published by the French government, in 1869.

2. What is believed to be the second part of the Codex Troano, now (1882) in process of publication in Paris.

3. The Codex Peresianus, in the National Library, Paris, a very limited edition of which has been issued.

[1] "Se les quemamos todos lo qual à maravilla sentian y les dava pena." *Relacion de las Cosas de Yucatan, p. 316.*

4. The Dresden Codex, in Kingsborough's Mexico, and photographed in colors, to the number of 50 copies, in 1880, which is believed to contain fragments of two different manuscripts.

To these are, perhaps, to be added one other in Europe and two in Mexico, which are in private hands, and are alleged to be of the same character.

All the above are distinctly in characters which were peculiar to the Mayas, and which are clearly variants of those found on the sculptured beams and slabs of Uxmal, Chichen Itza, Palenque and Copan.

It is possible that many other manuscripts may be discovered in time, for Landa tells us that it was the custom to bury with the priests the books which they had written. As their tombs were at times of solid stones, firmly cemented together, and well calculated to resist the moisture and other elements of destruction for centuries, it is nowise unlikely that explorations in Yucatan will bring to light some of these hidden documents.

The contents of these books, so far as we can judge from the hints in the early writers, related chiefly to the ritual and calendar, to their history or Katuns, to astrological predictions and divinations, to their mythology, and to their system of healing disease.

§ 9. *Modern Maya Manuscripts.*

As I have said, the Mayas were naturally a literary people. Had they been offered the slightest chance for the cultivation of their intellects they would have become a nation of readers and writers. Striking testimony to this effect is offered by Doctor Don Augustin de Echano, Prebend of the Cathedral Church of Merida, about the middle of the last century. He observes that twelve years of experience among the Indians had taught him that they were very desirous of knowledge, and that as soon as they learned to read, they eagerly perused everything they could lay their hands on; and as they had nothing in their tongue but some old writings that treated of sorceries and quackeries, the worthy Prebend thought it an excellent idea that they should be supplied, in place of these, with some —— *sermons!*[1] But what else could be expected of a body of men who crushed out with equal bigotry every spark of mental independence in their own country?

[1] "La experiencia de manejar tan incessantemente à los Indios en cerca de doce años que los servi, me enseñó, que el motivo de estar todavia muchos tan pegados à sus antiguedades, era porque siendo los naturales muy curiosòs, y aplicandose à saber leer: los que esto logran. quanto papel tienen à mano, tanto leen: y no aviendo entre ella, mas tratados en su idioma, que los que sus antepasados escribieron, cuya materia es solo de sus hechice-

The "old writings" to which the Prebend alludes
were composed by natives who had learned to
write the Maya in the alphabet adopted by the
early missionaries and conquerors. An official
document in Maya, still extant, dates from 1542,
and from that time on there were natives who
wrote their tongue with fluency. But their favorite compositions were works similar to those to
which their forefathers had been partial, prophecies, chronicles and medical treatises.

Relying on their memories, and no doubt aided
by some of the ancient hieroglyphical manuscripts,
carefully secreted from the vandalism of the monks,
they wrote out what they could recollect of their
national literature.

There were at one time a large number of these
records. They are referred to by Cogolludo,
Sanchez Aguilar and other early historians. Probably nearly every village had one, which in time
became to be regarded with superstitious vene-
ration.

rias, encantos, y curaciones con muchos abusos, y ensalmos; ya
se ve que en estos bebian insensiblemente el tosigo para vomitar
despues su malicia en otros muchos." *Aprobacion del Doctor D.
Augustin de Echano*, etc., to Dr. Don Francisco Eugenio Domin-
guez, *Platicas de los Principales Mysterios de Nvestra Sta Fee,
hechas en el Idioma Yucateco*. Mexico, 1758. This extremely
rare work is highly prized for the purity and elegance of the Maya
employed by the author.

Wherever written, each of these books bore the same name; it was always referred to as "The Book of Chilan Balam." To distinguish them apart, the name of the village where one was composed was added. Thus we have still preserved to us, in whole or in fragments, the Book of Chilan Balam of Chumayel, of Kaua, of Nabula, etc., in all, it is said, about sixteen.

"Chilan Balam" was the designation of a class of priests. "Chilan," says Bishop Landa, "was the name of their priests, whose duty it was to teach the sciences, to appoint holy days, to treat the sick, to offer sacrifices, and especially to utter the oracles of the gods. They were so highly honored by the people that usually they were carried on litters on the shoulders of the devotees."[1] Strictly speaking, in Maya, *chilan* means "interpreter," "mouth-piece," from " *chij*," " the mouth," and in this ordinary sense frequently occurs in other writings. The word *balam*—literally, " tiger,"— was also applied to a class of priests, and is still in use among the natives of Yucatan as the designation of the protective spirits of fields and towns, as I have shown at length in a study of the word

[1] *Relacion de las Cosas de Yucatan*, page 160.

as it occurs in the native myths of Guatemala.[1]
" *Chilan Balam*," therefore, is not a proper name,
but a title, and in ancient times designated the
priest who announced the will of the gods and
explained the sacred oracles. This accounts for
the universality of the name and the sacredness
of its associations.

The dates of the books which have come down
to us are various. One of them, " The Book of
Chilan Balam of Mani," was undoubtedly composed not later than 1595, as is proved by internal
evidence. Various passages in the works of
Landa, Lizana, Sanchez Aguilar and Cogolludo—
all early historians of Yucatan—prove that many
of these native manuscripts existed in the sixteenth
century. Several rescripts date from the seventeenth century—most from the latter half of the
eighteenth.

The names of the writers are generally not
given, probably because the books, as we have
them, are all copies of older manuscripts, with

[1] *The Names of the Gods in the Kiche Myths of Central America. Proceedings of the American Philosophical Society*, Vol.
XIX, 1881. The terminal letter in both these words—"*chilan*,"
" *balam*,"—may be either " *n*" or " *m*," the change being one of
dialect and local pronunciation. I have followed the older
authorities in writing "*Chilan Balam*," the modern preferring
"*Chilam Balam*."

merely the occasional addition of current items of note by the copyist; as, for instance, a malignant epidemic which prevailed in the peninsula in 1673 is mentioned as a present occurrence by the copyist of " The Book of Chilan Balam of Nabula."

These " Books of Chilan Balam" are the principal sources from which Señor Pio Perez derived his knowledge of the ancient Maya system of computing time, and also drew what he published concerning the history of the Mayas before the Conquest, and from them also are taken the various chronicles which I present in the present volume.

That I am enabled to do so is due to the untiring researches of Dr. Carl Hermann Berendt, who visited Yucatan four times, in order to study the native language, to examine the antiquities of the peninsula, and to take accurate copies, often in fac-simile, of as many ancient manuscripts as he could discover. After his death, his collection came into my hands.

The task of deciphering these manuscripts is by no means a light one, and I must ask in advance for considerable indulgence for my attempt. Words and phrases are used which are not explained in the dictionaries, or, if explained, are used in a different sense from that now current.

The orthography is far from uniform, each syllable is often written separately, and as the punctuation is wholly fanciful or entirely absent, the separation of words, sentences and paragraphs is often uncertain and the meaning obscure.

Another class of documents are the titles to the municipal lands, the records of surveys, etc. I have copies of several of these, and among them was found the history of the Conquest, by Nakuk Pech, which I publish. It was added to the survey of his town, as a general statement of his rights and defence of the standing of his family.

My translations are not in flowing and elegant language. Had they been so, they would not have represented the originals. For the sake of accuracy I have not hesitated to sacrifice the requirements of English composition.

§ *10. Grammars and Dictionaries of the Language.*

The learned Yucatecan, Canon Crescencio Carillo y Ancona, states in his last work that there have been written thirteen grammars and seventeen dictionaries of the Maya.[1]

The first grammar printed was that of Father Luis de Villalpando. This early missionary died in 1551 or 1552, and his work was not issued until

---

[1] *Historia Antigua de Yucatan, p. 123* (Merida, 1882).

some years later. Father Juan Coronel also gave
a short Maya grammar to the press, together
with a *Doctrina*. It is believed that copies of both
of these are preserved. Beltran, however, ac-
knowledges that in preparing his own grammar
he has never seen either of these earlier
works.[1]

In 1684, the *Arte de la Lengua Maya*, composed
by Father Gabriel de San Buenaventura, a French
Franciscan stationed in Yucatan, was printed in
Mexico.[2] Only a few copies of this work are
known. It has, however, been reprinted, though
not with a desirable fidelity, by the Abbe Brasseur
(de Bourbourg), in the second volume of the
reports of the *Mission Scientifique au Mexique et
à l'Amerique Centrale*, Paris, 1870.

The leading authority on Maya grammar is
Father Pedro Beltran, who was a native of Yucatan, and instructor in the Maya language in the
convent of Merida about 1740. He was thoroughly
conversant with the native tongue, and his *Arte*

---

[1] *Arte del Idioma Maya*, p. 242 (2d ed).

[2] *Arte de la Lengua Maya*, compuesto por el R. P. Fr. Gabriel
de San Buenaventura Predicador y difinidor habitual de la Provincia de San Joseph de Yucathan del Orden de N. P. S. Francisco. Año de 1684. Con licencia; En Mexico, por la Viuda de
Bernardo Calderon, 4to. pag. 1-4, leaves 5-41.

F

was reprinted in Merida, in 1859, as the best work
of the kind which had been produced.[1]

The eminent antiquary, Don Juan Pio Perez
contemplated writing a Maya grammar, and collected a number of notes for that purpose,[2] as did
also the late Dr. Berendt, but neither brought his
work to any degree of completeness. I have copies
of the notes left by both these diligent students,
as also both editions of Beltran, and an accurate
MS. copy of Buenaventura, from all of which I
have derived assistance in completing the present
study.

The first Maya dictionary printed was issued in
the City of Mexico in 1571. It was published as
that of Father Luis de Villalpando, but as he had
then been dead nearly twenty years, it was probably merely based upon his vocabulary. It was in
large 4to, of the same size as the second edition
of Molina's *Vocabulario de la Lengua Mexicana.*
At least one copy of it is known to be in existence.

---

[1] *Arte del Idioma Maya reducido a succintas reglas, y semi-
lexicon Yucateco* por el R. P. F. Pedro Beltran de Santa Rosa
Maria. En Mexico por la Viuda de D. Joseph Bernardo de
Hogal. Año de 1746. 8vo, pp. 8, 1-188. Segunda edicion, Mérida de Yucatan, Imprenta de J. D. Espinosa. Julio, 1859. 8vo,
9 leaves, pp. 242.

[2] *Apuntes para una Gramatica Maya.* Por Don Juan Pio Perez,
pp. 45-136. *MSS.*

For more than three centuries no other dictionary
was put to press, although for some unexplained
reason that of Villalpando was unknown in Yucatan.   At length, in 1877, the publication was completed at Mérida, of the *Diccionario de la Lengua
Maya*, by Don Juan Pio Perez.[1]   It contains about
20,000 words, and is Maya-Spanish only.   It is the
result of a conscientious and lifelong study of the
language, and a work of great merit. The deficien-
cies it presents are, that it does not give the principal parts of the verbs, that it omits or does not
explain correctly many old terms in the language,
and that it gives very few examples of idioms or
phrases showing the uses of words and the construction of sentences.

I can say little in praise of the *Vocabulaire
Maya-Francais-Espagnole*, compiled by the Abbé
Brasseur (de Bourbourg), and printed in the
second volume of the Report of the *Mission Scientifique au Mexique et à l'Amerique Centrale*.   It
contains about ten thousand words, but many of
these are drawn from doubtful sources, and are
incorrectly given ; while the derivations and anal-

---

[1] *Diccionario de la Lengua Maya*, por D. Juan Pio Perez. Merida
de Yucatan.   Imprenta literaria, de Juan F. Molina Solis, 1866–
1877.   Large 8vo, two cols. pp. i–xx, 1–437.

ogies proposed are of a character unknown to the
science of language.

Besides the above and various vocabularies of
minor interest, I have made use of three manuscript dictionaries of the first importance, which
were obtained by the late Dr. Berendt. They
belonged to three Franciscan convents which
formerly existed in Yucatan, and as they are all
anonymous, I shall follow Dr. Berendt's example,
and refer to them by the names of the convents to
which they belonged. These were the convent of
San Francisco in Merida, that at the town of Ticul
and that at Motul.

The most recent of these is that of the convent
of Ticul. It bears the date 1690, and is in two
parts, Spanish-Maya and Maya-Spanish.

The *Diccionario del Convento de San Francisco
de Merida* bears no date, but in the opinion of the
most competent scholars who have examined it,
among them Señor Pio Perez, it is older than that
of Ticul, probably by half a century. It is also in
two parts, which have evidently been prepared, by
different hands.

The Diccionario del Convento de Motul is by far
the most valuable of the three, and has not been
known to Yucatecan scholars. A copy of it was

picked up on a book stall in the City of Mexico by the Abbé Brasseur, and sold by him to Mr. John Carter Brown, of Providence, R. I. In 1864 this was very carefully copied by Dr. Berendt, who also made extensive additions to it from other sources, indicating such by the use of inks of different colors. This copy, in three large quarto volumes, in all counting over 2500 pages, is that which I now have, and have found of indispensable assistance in solving some of the puzzles presented by the ancient texts in the present volume.

The particular value of the *Diccionario de Motul* is not merely the richness of its vocabulary and its numerous examples of construction, but that it presents the language as it was when the Spaniards first arrived. The precise date of its compilation is indeed not given, but the author speaks of a comet which he saw in 1577, and gives other evidence that he was writing in the first generation after the Conquest.

THE CHRONICLES.

I. THE SERIES OF THE KATUNS.
From the Book of Chilan Balam of Mani.

II. THE SERIES OF THE KATUNS.
From the Book of Chilan Balam of Tizimin.

III. THE RECORD OF THE COUNT OF THE KATUNS.
From the Book of Chilan Balam of Chumayel.

IV. THE MAYA KATUNS.
From the Book of Chilan Balam of Chumayel.

V. THE CHIEF KATUNS.
From the Book of Chilan Balam of Chumayel.

THE CHRONICLES.

The chronicles and fragments of chronicles which I have collected here are all taken from the various "Books of Chilan Balam." They constitute about all that remains to us, so far as I know, of the ancient history of the peninsula. There are, indeed, in other portions of these "Books" references to historical events before the Conquest, but no other consecutive narrations of them.

Except the one given first, none of these has ever been printed, nor even translated from the Maya into any European language. Whether they corroborate or contradict one another, it is equally important for American archæology to have them preserved and presented in their original form.

It does not come within my present purpose to try to reconcile the discrepancies between them. I am furnishing materials for history, not writing it, and my chief duty is to observe accuracy, even at the risk of depreciating the value of the documents I offer.

I have, therefore, followed strictly the manuscripts which I possess in fac-similes of the originals, and when I believe the text is corrupt or in
error, I have suggested apart from the text what
I suppose to be the needed correction to the
passage.

In the notes I have also discussed such grammatical or historical questions as have occurred
to me as of use in elucidating the text.

There will be found considerable repetition in
these different versions, as must necessarily be
from their character, if they have a claim to be
authentic records ; but it is also fair to add that
details will be found in each which are omitted in
the others, and hence, that all are valuable.

This similarity may be explained by two suppo-
sitions ; either they are copies from a common
original, or they present the facts they narrate in
general formulæ which had been widely adopted
by the priests for committing to memory their
ancient history. The differences which we find in
them preclude the former hypothesis except as it
may apply to the first two. The similarities in
the others I believe are no more than would occur
in relating the same incidents which had been
learned through fixed forms of narration.

The division into sections I have made for convenience of reference. The variants I have given at the bottom of the page are readings which I think are preferable to those in the text, or corrections of manifest errors; but I have endeavored to give the text, just as it is in the best MSS. I have, errors and all.

It is not my purpose to enter into a critical historical analysis of these chronicles. But a few remarks may be made to facilitate their examination.

Making the necessary omissions in No. II, which I point out in the prefatory note to it, it will be found that all five agree tolerably well in the length of time they embrace. Nos. III and IV begin at a later date than the others, but coincide as far as they go.

The total period of time, from the earliest date given, to the settlement of the country by the Spaniards, is 71 katuns. If the katun is estimated at twenty years, this equals 1420 years; if at twenty-four years, then we have 1704 years.

All the native writers agree, and I think, in spite of the contrary statement of Bishop Landa, that we may look upon it as beyond doubt, that the last day of the 11th katun was July 15th, 1541.

Therefore the one of the above calculations would carry us back to A. D. 121, the other to B. C. 173.

The chief possibility of error in the reckoning would be from confusing the great cycles of 260 (or 312) years, one with another, and assigning events to different cycles which really happened in the same.   This would increase the number of the cycles, and thus extend the period of time they appear to cover.   This has undoubtedly been done in No. II.

According to the reckoning as it now stands, six complete great cycles were counted, and parts of two others, so that the native at the time of the Conquest would have had eight great cycles to distinguish apart.

I have not found any clear explanation how this was accomplished.   We do not even know what name was given to this great cycle, nor whether the calendar was sufficiently perfected to prevent confusion in dates in the remote past.

I find, however, two passages in the collection of ancient manuscripts, which I have before referred to as the *Codice Perez*, which seem to have a bearing on this point ; but as the text is somewhat corrupt and several of the expressions archaic, I am not certain that I catch the right meaning. These passages are as follows:—

U hiɔil lahun ahau u ɔocol hun uuɔ katun, u zut tucaten oxlahunpiz katun ɔiban tu uichob tu pet katun; la hun uuɔ katun u kaba ca bin ɔococ u·than lae, u hoppol tucaten; bay hoppci ca ɔib lae ca tun culac u yanal katun lae. Cabin ɔococ uaxac ahau lae u hoppol tucaten lae. (Page 90.)

U hiɔil Lahun Ahau u ɔocol u nuppul oxlahunpez katun ɔiban u uichob tu pet tzaton lo hun (*sic*) uuɔ katun u kaba ca bin ɔococ u than lae, ca tun culac u yanal katun ca bin ɔococ uaxac Ahau lae; hu hoppol tucaten bay hoppci ca ɔib. (Page 168.)

Translation.

At the last of the tenth ahau katun is ended one doubling of the katun, and the return a second time of thirteen katuns is written on the face of the katun circle; one doubling of the katuns, as it is called, will then finish its course, to begin again; and when it begins, it is written that another katun commences: when the eighth katun ends it begins again (*i. e.,* to count with this eighth as the first of the next " doubling").

At the last of the tenth Ahau Katun is ended the joining together of thirteen katuns (which is) written on the face of the katun circle; one doubling of the katuns, as it ·is called, will then finish its course, and another katun will begin and will end as the eighth katun; this begins a second time, as it began (at first) and was then written.

In other words, if I do not miss the writer's meaning, the repetitions of the great cycle of thirteen katuns were not counted from either of its terminals, to wit, the thirteenth or the second katun, but from the tenth katun. These repetitions were

called *uuɔ katun*, the doubling or foldings over of
the katuns, and they were inscribed on the circle
or wheel of the katuns at that part of it where the
tenth katun was entered. These wheels were
called *u pet katun*, the circle of the katuns, or *u
met katun*, the wheel of the katuns, or *u uazaklom
katun*, the return of the katuns. I have several
copies of them, and one is given in Landa's work,
but I know of none which is a genuine original,
and, therefore, it is not surprising that I do not find
on any of them the signs referred to adjacent to
the tenth katun.

For the convenience of the reader I have drawn
up the following chronological table of the events
referred to in the Chronicles, arranging them
under the Great Cycles and Katuns to which they
would belong were the former numbered according to the regular sequence given on page 59. I
have also inserted the katuns which were omitted
by the native chroniclers, but which, according to
that sequence, are necessary in order to complete
their records in accordance with the theory of the
Maya calendar. The references in Roman numerals are to the different chronicles.

SYNOPSIS OF MAYA CHRONOLOGY.

Great Cycle.	*Katun.*	
I.	8	They leave Nonoual (I.)
	6	
	4	
	2	
II.	13	They arrive at Chacnouitan (I.)
	11	
	9	
	7	
	5	
	3	
	1	
	12	
	10	
	8	Chichen Itza heard of (II.)
	6	Bacalar and Chichen Itza discovered (I, II, III.)
	4	Ahmekat Tutulxiu arrives (I ?, II.)
	2	
III.	13	*Pop* first counted (*i. e.* calendar arranged) (II, III.)
	11	Remove to Chichen Itza (I.)
	9	
	7	
	5	
	3	
	1	Abandon Chichen Itza ; remove to Champoton (I, II.)
	12	
	10	Abandon Chichen Itza ; remove to Champoton (III.)
	8	
	6	Champoton taken (I, II.)
	4	Champoton taken (III.)
	2	
IV.	13	
	11	
	9	
	7	
	5	
	3	
	1	
	12	
	10	
	8	Champoton abandoned (I, II, III.)
	6	The Itzas houseless (I. II, III.) The well dressed " driven out (IV.)

	4	Return to Chichen Itza (I, II.)
	2	Uxmal founded (I.) The League in Mayapan begins (I.)
V.	13	Mayapan founded (V.)
	11	
	9	
	7	
	5	Chichen Itza destroyed by Kinich Kakmo (IV.)
	3	
	1	The last of the Itzas leave Chichen Itza (IV.)
	12	
	10	Uxmal founded (II.)
	8	Plot of or against Hunac Ceel (I, II, III.) Zaclactun Mayapan founded (IV.) Chakanputun burned (IV.)
	6	War with Ulmil (I.)
	4	The land of Mayapan seized (II, III.)
	2	
VI.	13	
	11	Mayapan attacked by Itzas under Ulmil and depopulated by foreigners (I.)
	9	
	7	
	5	Naked cannibals came (IV.)
	3	
	1	Tancah Mayapan destroyed (IV.)
	12	
	10	
	8	Mayapan finally destroyed (I, II, III, V.)
	6	The Maya league ended (V.)
	4	The pestilence (II, III, IV.)
	2	Spaniards first seen (I, II.) Smallpox (III.)
VII.	13	Ahpula died (I, II, III.) The pestilence (I.)
	11	Spaniards arrive (I, II, III, IV, V.) Ahpula died (IV.).

I. THE SERIES OF THE KATUNS.

From the Book of Chilan Balam of Mani.

The first chronicle which I present is the only one which has been heretofore published. On account of its comparative fullness it deserves especial attention. It is taken from the Book of Chilan Balam of the town of Mani.

This town, according to a tradition preserved by Herrera, was founded after the destruction of Mayapan, and, therefore, not more than seventy years before the arrival of the Spaniards. Mayapan was destroyed in consequence of a violent feud between the two powerful families who jointly ruled there, the Cocoms and the Xius or Tutul Xius. The latter, having slain all members of the Cocom family to be found in the city, deserted its site and removed south about fifteen miles, and there established as their capital a city to which they gave the name Mani, "which means 'it is past,' as if to say 'let us start anew.'"[1]

[1] "No lo pudiendo sufrir los otros Señores, se conjuraron con el Señor de los Tutuxius, i acudiendo en Dia señalado à la Casa del Señor Cocom, le mataron con sus Hijos, salvo uno, que estaba

At the time of the Conquest the reigning chief of the Tutulxius was friendly to the Spaniards, and voluntarily submitted to their rule, as we are informed with much minuteness of detail by the historian Cogolludo.[1] We may reasonably suppose, therefore, that this chronicle was brought from Mayapan in the " Books of Science," which Herrera refers to as esteemed their greatest treasure by the chiefs who broke up their ancient confederation when Mayapan was deserted.   Hence the records ran a better chance of being preserved in this province than in those which were desolated by war.   As I have already said (page 65) a large number were destroyed precisely at Mani by Bishop Landa, in 1562.

I find among the memoranda of Dr. Berendt

ausente, i le saquearon la Casa, i le tomaron sus Heredades, i desamparon la Ciudad [de Mayapan], deseando cada Señor vivir en libertad en sus Pueblos, al cabo de quinientos Años, que se fundò, en la qual havian vivido con mucha Policia; i havria que se despoblò, segun la cuenta de los Indios, hasta que llegaron los Castellanos à Yucatàn, setenta Años. Cada Señor procurò de llevar los mas Libros de sus Ciencias, que pudò, à su Tierra, adonde hicieron Templos; i esta es la principal causa de los muchos Edificios, que hai en Yucatan. Siguiò toda su gente Ahxiui, Señor de los Tutuxius, i poblò en Mani, que quiere decir, ià pasò; como si dixese, hagamos Libro nuevo; i de tal manera poblaron sus Pueblos, que hicieron una gran Provincia, que se llama oi dia, Tutuxiù."   Herrera, *Historia de las Indias Occidentales*, Dec. IV, Lib. X, caps. II, III.

[1] *Historia de Yucatan*, Lib. III, cap. VI.

reference to four "Books of Chilan Balam," of Mani. These dated from 1689, 1697, 1755 and 1761, respectively, but I have not learned from which of these Pio Perez extracted the chronicles he gave Mr. John L. Stephens. Dr. Berendt adds that it was from one which was in possession of a native schoolmaster of Mani, who, having the surname Balam, claimed to be descended from the original Chilan Balam ! [1]

The first publication of the document was in the Appendix to the second volume of Mr. Stephens' *Incidents of Travel in Yucatan* (New York, 1843). It included the original Maya text, with a not very accurate translation into English of Pio Perez's rendering of the Maya. From Mr. Stephen's volume, the document has been copied into various publications in Mexico, Yucatan and Europe.

[1] I quote Dr. Berendt's words. "Los datos historicós que publicò Stephens en el Apendice de su obra fueron extractados de tal libro de Chilam Balam en poder de un Indio de Mani, maestro de escuela, que por tener el mismo apelido Balam pretendió ser descendiente del sacerdote de los Mayas que llegó à padrinar esta clase de escritos." *Chilam Balam, Articulos y Fragmentos en Lengua Maya* MSS., Advertencia, p. VII.

I have also in my collection a manuscript copy of what Yucatecan scholars call the *Codice Perez*, a mass of materials copied by Señor Pio Perez, among them this chronicle. The following is his own note at its close :—

"Hasta aqui termina el libro titulado Chilambalam que se conserva en el Pueblo de Mani en poder del maestro de Capilla."

The other attempt at an independent translation was that of the Abbé Brasseur (de Bourbourg), published at Paris in 1864, in the same
volume with Landa's *Relacion de las Cosas de
Yucatan.* The text he took from Stephens' book,
errors and omissions included, and his translation
is entirely based on the English one, as he evidently did not have access to the original Spanish
of Pio Perez.

The most important recent study of the subject
has been made by Dr. Valentini, who published
the notes of Pio Perez on his translation, and gave
a general re-examination of ancient Maya history,
with a great deal of sagacity and a large acquaint-
ance with the related Spanish literature.[1]   He is,
however, in error in stating that he was the first to
publish the notes of Perez, as they had previously
been printed in a work by Canon Carrillo.[2]

Much use of this chronicle has been made by the
recent historians of Yucatan, Don Eligio Ancona

[1] *The Katunes of Maya History,* A Chapter in the Early Chronology of Central America, with special reference to the Pio Perez
Manuscripts.   By Philip J. J. Valentini, Ph. D.   *Proceedings of
the American Antiquarian Society,* 1879. (Worcester, Mass.
Press of Charles Hamilton, 1880).   The reprint is 60 pages, octavo.

[2] Crescencio Carrillo, *Manual de Historia y Geografía de la
Peninsula de Yucatan,* pp. 16-27.   (12mo : Merida de Yucatan ;
imprenta de J. D. Espinosa e Hijos.)

and the Canon Crescencio Carrillo y Ancona ; but I am surprised to find that they have depended entirely on the previous labors of Pio Perez, Stephens and Brasseur, and have made no attempt to verify or extend them.

Dr. Berendt, although earnestly devoted to collecting and copying these records did not, as Dr. Valentini observes, ever attempt a translation of any of them.

No hint is given as to the author of the document, nor do we know from what sources he derived his information. It has been plausibly suggested that it was an epitome of the history of their nations, which was learned by heart and handed down from master to disciple, and which served as a verbal key to the interpretation of the painted and sculptured records, and to the "katun stones" which were erected at the expiration of each cycle and inscribed with the principal events which had transpired in it.

The Abbé Brasseur placed at the head of his edition of this chronicle the title, in Maya:—

"LELO LAI U TZOLAN KATUNIL TI MAYAB," which he translates—

"SÉRIES DES EPOQUES DE L'HISTOIRE MAYA."

This is an invention of the learned antiquary.

There is no such nor any other title to the original. It is simply called in the first line *u tzolan katun*, the arrangement or order of the katuns. The word *tzolan* is a verbal noun, the past participle of the passive voice of *tzol*, which means to put in order, to arrange, and is in the genitive of the thing possessed, as indicated by the pronoun *u*. Literally, the phrase reads, "their arrangement (the) katuns."

1. Lai u tzolan katun lukci ti cab ti yotoch Nonoual cante anilo Tutulxiu ti chikin Zuiua u luumil u talelob Tulapan 'chiconahthan.

2. Cante bin ti katun lic u ximbalob ca uliob uaye yetel Holon Chantepeuh yetel u cuchulob. Ca hokiob ti petene uaxac ahau bin yan cuchi uac ahau, can ahau, cabil ahau, cankal haab catac hunppel haab, tumen hun piztun oxlahun ahau cuchie, ca uliob uay ti petene, cankal haab catac hunppel haab, tu pakteil, yetel cu ximbalob lukci tu luumilob ca talob uay ti petene Chacnouitan lae; u añoil lae 81 —— —— —— 81.

3. Uaxac ahau, uac ahau; cabil ahau kuchci chacnouitan Ahmekat Tutulxiu; hunppel haab minan ti hokal haab cuchi yanob chacnouitan lae; lai u habil lae —— —— —— 99 años.

4. Laitun uchci u chicpahal tzucubte Ziyan caan lae Bakhalal; can ahau, cabil ahau, oxlahun ahau, oxkal haab cu tepalob Ziyan caan ca emob uay

¹ chichcunahthan.

95

lae; lai u habil cu tepalob Bakhalal [1] chuulte laitun
chicpahci Chichen Itza lae ——— ——— 60 años.

5. Buluc ahau, bolon ahau, uuc ahau, ho ahau,
ox ahau, hun ahau, uackal haab, cu tepalob Chichen
Itzaa, ca paxi Chichen Itza, ca binob cahtal Chanputun, ti yanhi u yotochob ah Itzaob kuyan uincob lae; lay u habil lae ——— ——— 120.

6. Uac ahau chucuc u luumil Chanputun. Can
ahau, cabil ahau, oxlahun ahau, buluc ahau, bolon
ahau, uuc ahau, ho ahau, ox ahau, hun ahau, lahca
ahau, lahun ahau, uaxac ahau paxci Chanputun;
oxlahunkal haab cu tepalob Chanputun tumenel
Ytza uinicob ca talob u tzac le u yotochob tu caten;
laixtun u katunil binciob ah Itzaob yalan che,
yalan [2] aban, yalan ak ti numyaob lae; lai u habil
cu [3] xinbal lae ——— ——— ——— 260.

7. Uac ahau, can ahau, cakal haab, ca talob u
heɔob yotoch tu caten ca tu zatahob chakanputun;
lay u habil lae ——— ——— ——— 40.

8. Lai u katunil cabil ahau u heɔcicab Ahcuitok
Tutulxiu Uxmal; cabil ahau, oxlahun ahau, buluc
ahau, bolon ahau, uuc ahau, ho ahau, ox ahau, hun
ahau, lahca ahau, lahun ahau; lahun kal haab cu
tepalob yetel u halach uinicil chichen Itza yetel
Mayalpan; lai u habil lae ——— ——— 200.

---

[1] uchuc.   [2] haban.   [3] ximbal.

9. Lai u katunil buluc ahau bolon ahau uuc
ahau, uaxac ahau, paxci u halach uinicil Chichen
Itzaa tumenel u kebanthan Hunac eel; ca uch
ti Chacxibchac Chichen Itzaa tu kebanthan Hunac
eel u halach uinicil Mayalpan ich paae. Cankal
haab catac lahunpiz haab, tu lahun tun, uaxac
ahau cuchie lai u habil paxci tumenel Ahzinteyut
chan yetel Tzuntecum, yetel Taxcal, yetel Pantemit, Xuchueuet yetel Ytzcuat, yetel Kakaltecat;
lai u kaba uiniclob lae uuctulob ah Mayelpanob
lae ———— ———— ———— ———— 90.

10. Laili u katunil uaxac ahau lai ca binob u
paa ah Ulmil ahau tumenel u uahal uahoob yetel
ah Itzmal ulil ahau lae oxlahun uuɔ u katunilob ca paxob tumen Hunac eel; tumenel u
ɔabal u natob; uac ahau ca ɔoci hunkal haab catac
canlahun pizi; lai u habil cu 'xinbal — 34.

11. Uac ahau, can ahau, cabil ahau, oxlahun
ahau, buluc ahau chucuc u luumil ich paa Mayapan,
tumenel u pach tulum, tumenel multepal ich cah
Mayalpan, tumenel Ytza uinicob yetel Ulmil
ahau lae, cankal haab catac oxppel haab;
yocol buluc ahau cuchi paxci Mayalpan tumenel
ahuitzil ɔul tan cah Mayapan ———— ———— 83.

12. Uaxac ahau lai paxci Mayapan; lay u katunil

¹ ximbal.

uac ahau, can ahau, cabil ahau, lai haab, cu ximbal
ca yax mani españoles u yax ulci caa luumi
Yucatan tzucubte lae oxkal haab paxac ichpaa
cuchie ———— ———— ———— ———— 60.

13. Oxlahun ahau, buluc ahau uchci mayacimil
ich paa yetel nohkakil; oxlahun ahau cimci Ahpula;
uacppel haab u binel ma ɔococ u xocol oxlahun
ahau cuchie; ti yanil u xocol haab ti lakin cuchie,
canil kan cumlahi pop, tu holhun zip catac oxppeli,
bolon imix u kinil lai cimci Ahpula; laytun año cu
ximbal cuchi lae ca oheltab lai u xoc *numeroil anos*
lae 1536 años cuchie, oxkal haab paxac ichpa cuchi
lae.

14. Laili ma ɔococ u xocol buluc ahau lae lai
ulci *españoles* kul uincob ti lakin, u talob ca uliob
uay tac luumil lae; bolon ahau hoppci *cristianoil;*
uchci caputzihil; laili ichil u katunil lae ulci yax
obispo Toroba u kaba; heix año cu ximbal uchie
1544.

15. Yan cuchi uuc ahau cimci yax obispo de
landa; ychil u katunil ho ahau ca yan cahi padre
manii lai año lae ———— ———— ———— 1550.

16. Lai año cu ximbal ca cahi padre yok haa
1552.

17. Lai año cu ximbal ca uli Oidor la ca paki Es-
pital ———— ———— ———— ———— 1559.

18. Lai año cu ximbal ca kuchi Doctor Quijada yax gob⁰ʳ uaye —— —— —— 1560.

19. Lai año cu ximbal ca uchci c̃uitab lae

1562.

20. Lai año cu ximbal ca uli Mariscal gob⁰ʳ ca betab ' thulub —— —— —— 1563.

21. Lai año cu ximbal ca uchci nohkakil lae

1609.

22. Lai año cu ximbal ca hichiucal kaxob 1610.

23. Lai año cu ximbal ca ɔibtah cah tumenel Juez Diego Pareja 1611.

¹ chulub.

TRANSLATION.

1. This is the arrangement of the katuns since the departure was made from the land, from the house Nonoual, where were the four Tutulxiu, from Zuiva at the west; they came from the land Tulapan, having formed a league.

2. Four katuns had passed in which they journeyed when they arrived here with Holon Chantepeuh and his followers. When they set out for this country it was the eighth ahau. The sixth ahau, the fourth ahau, the second ahau (passed), four score years and one year, for it was the first year of the thirteenth ahau when they arrived here in this country; four score years and one year in all had passed since they departed from the land and came here, to the province Chacnouitan. These were years   81.

3. The eighth ahau, the sixth ahau; in the second ahau Ahmekat Tutulxiu arrived at Chacnouitan; they were in Chacnouitan five score years lacking one year; these were years   99.

4. Then took place the discovery of the pro-

vince Ziyan caan or Bakhalal; the fourth ahau, the second ahau, the thirteenth ahau, three score years they ruled Ziyan caan when they descended here: in these years that they ruled Bakhalal it occurred then that Chichen Itza was discovered. 60 years.

5. The eleventh ahau, the ninth ahau, the seventh ahau, the fifth ahau, the third ahau, the first ahau, six score years, they ruled at Chichen Itza; then they abandoned Chichen Itza and went to live at Chanputun; there those of Itza, holy men, had their houses; these were years   120.

6. In the sixth ahau the land of Chanputun was seized. The fourth ahau, the second ahau, the thirteenth ahau, the eleventh ahau, the ninth ahau, the seventh ahau, the fifth ahau, the third ahau, the first ahau, the twelfth ahau, the tenth ahau; the eighth ahau Chanputun was abandoned; thirteen score years Chanputun was ruled by the Itza men when they came in search of their houses a second time; in this katun those of Itza were under the trees, under the boughs, under the branches, to their sorrow; the years that passed were   260.

7. The sixth ahau, the fourth ahau, two score years, (had passed) when they came and estab-

lished their houses a second time, and they lost
Chakanputun; these were years   40.

8. In the katun the second ahau Ahcuitok Tutulxiu founded (the city of) Uxmal; the second
ahau, the thirteenth ahau, the eleventh ahau, the
ninth ahau, the seventh ahau, the fifth ahau, the
third ahau, the first ahau, the twelfth ahau, the
tenth ahau; ten score years they ruled with the
governor of Chichen Ytza and Mayapan; these
were years   200.

9. Then were the katuns eleventh ahau, ninth
ahau, sixth ahau; in the eighth ahau the governor
of Chichen Itza was driven out on account of his
plotting against Hunac Eel; and this happened
to Chac Xib Chac of Chichen Itza on account of
his plotting against Hunac Eel the governor of
Mayapan, the fortress. Four score years and ten
years, and it was the tenth year of the eighth ahau
that it was depopulated by Ah Zinteyut Chan,
with Tzuntecum, and Taxcal, and Pantemit, Xuchueuet and Ytzcuat and Kakaltecat: these were
the names of the seven men of Mayapan   90.

10. In this eighth ahau they went to the fortress
of the ruler of Ulmil on account of his banquet
to Ulil ruler of Itzmal; they were thirteen divisions of warriors when they were dispersed by

Hunac Eel, in order that they might know what was to be given ; in the sixth ahau it ended, one score years and fourteen ; the years that passed were   34.

11. The sixth ahau, the fourth ahau, the second ahau, the thirteenth ahau, the eleventh ahau ; then was invaded the land of the fortress of Mayapan by the men of Itza and their ruler Ulmil on account of the seizure of the castle by the joint government in the city of Mayapan ; four score years and three years ; the eleventh ahau had entered when Mayapan was depopulated by foreigners from the mountains in the midst of the city of Mayapan   83.

12. In the eighth ahau Mayapan was depopulated ; then were the sixth ahau, the fourth ahau, the second ahau ; during this year the Spaniards first passed and first came to this land the province of Yucatan, sixty years after the fortress was depopulated. ——   ——   ——   —— 60.

13. The thirteenth ahau ; the eleventh ahau took place the pestilence in the fortresses and the smallpox ; in the thirteenth ahau Ahpula died ; for six years the count of the thirteenth ahau will not be ended ; the count of the year was toward the East, the month Pop began with (the

day) fourth Kan ; the eighteenth day of the month
Zip (that is), 9 Imix, was the day on which Ahpula
died ; and that the count may be known in numbers and years it was the year 1536, sixty years
after the fortress was destroyed.

14. The count of the eleventh ahau was not
ended when the Spaniards, mighty men, arrived
from the east ; they came, they arrived here in this
land; the ninth ahau Christianity began ; baptism
took place ; also in this katun came the first bishop
Toroba by name; this was the year 1544.

15. In the seventh ahau died the first bishop de
Landa ; in the fifth katun the Fathers first settled
at Mani, in the year 1550.

16. As this year was passing the fathers settled
upon the water   ——   ——   —— 1552

17. As this year was passing the auditor came
and the hospital was built   ——   ——   1559

18. As this year was passing the first governor
Dr. Quijada, arrived here   ——   ——   1560

19. As this year was passing the hanging took
place   ——   ——   ——   —— 1562

20. As this year was passing the Governor Marshall came and built the reservoirs   —— 1563

21. As this year was passing the smallpox occurred   ——   ——   ——   —— 1609

22. As this year was passing those of Tekax were hanged　———　———　———　1610

23. As this year was passing the towns were written down by Judge Diego Pareja ——— 1611

NOTES.

1. The introductory paragraph is not less obscure in construction than it is important in its historical statements, and I shall give it, therefore, a particularly careful analysis.

I have already explained the term *u tzolan katun; lukci* is the aorist of *lukul*, which forms regularly *luki*, but the mutation to *ci* is used when the meaning *since* or *after that* is to be conveyed; as Beltran says, " cuando el verbo trae estos romances, *despues que ò desde que*, como este romance; despues que murio mi padre, estoy triste : *cimci in yume, okomuol*" (*Arte del Idioma Maya*, p. 61). *cab* means country or place, in the sense of residence, whereas *luum*, used in the same paragraph, is land or earth, in the general sense. The *Dicc. de Motul* says : " *cab*, pueblo ò region; *in cab*, mi pueblo, donde yo soy natural." *yotoch* is a compound of the possessive pronoun *u*, his or their, and *otoch*, the word for house when it is indicated whose house it is; otherwise *na* is used; *otoch* is probably allied to *och* a verbal root signifying to give food to, the house being looked upon as specifically the place where meals are prepared.

The word *cante* is translated by Perez and Brasseur as *four*, and applied to the Tutulxiu, while the intervening word *anilo* is not translated by either : *cante* is no doubt the numeral *four* with the numeral particle *te* suffixed. But here a serious difficulty arises. According to all the grammars and dictionaries the particle *te* is never used for counting persons,

106

but only "years, months, days (periods of time), leagues, cacao, eggs and gourds." Moreover, what is *anilo?* We have, indeed, the form *tenilo*, I am that one, from the particle *i* (Buenaventura, *Arte de la Lengua Maya*, fol. 27, verso); and we might have *yanilo*, they are those. But this necessitates a change in the text, and if that has to be done I should prefer to suppose that *anilo* was a mistake of the copyist, and that we should read *katun* or *katunile*. This would reconcile the numeral particle and would do away with the *four* Tutulxius, of whom we hear nothing afterwards.

chikin, the West, literally, that which bites or eats the sun, from *chi*, the mouth, and, as a verb, to bite. An eclipse is called in Maya *chibal kin*, the sun bitten; *ti chikin*, toward the West.

talelob, plural form of *tal* or *talel*, to come to, to go from.

chiconahthan is not translated by either Pio Perez or Brasseur, nor in that precise form has it any meaning. I take it, however, to be a faulty orthography for *chichcunahthan* which means to support that which another says, hence, to agree with, to act in concert with; *"chichcunah u thanil*, having renewed the agreement" (*Diccionario de Ticul*). It refers to an agreement entered into by the different leaders who were about to undertake the migration into unknown lands. Possibly, however, this is not a Maya word, but another echo of Aztec legend. *Chiconauhtlan*, "the place of the Nine," was a village and mountain north of the lake of Tezcuco and close to the sacred spot Teotiuacan, where, in Aztec myth, the gods assembled to create the sun and moon (Sahagun, *Historia de Nueva España*, Lib VII, cap. II). *Tulapan Chiconauhtlan* would thus become a compound local name.

It will be seen from the above that the translation which I have given of this paragraph does not satisfy me as certainly correct. I shall now give the original with an interlinear translation, and also those of Pio Perez and Brasseur, adding a free rendering which I am inclined to prefer, although it modifies the text somewhat.

Interlinear Translation.

Lai	u	tzolan	katun	lukci
This (is)	their	order	the katuns	since they departed

ti	cab,	ti	yotoch	Nonoual	cante
from the land		from	their house	Nonoual	the four

anilo,	Tutulxiu	ti.	chikin	Zuiua,
those the (?)	Tutulxiu	to	the West (of)	Zuiua

u	luumil	u	talelob	Tulapan	chiconah	than.
their	land (which)	they	came (from)	was Tulapan	acting in concert.	

Translation of Pio Perez.

Esta es la serie de Katunes corridos desde que se quitaron de la tierra y casa de Nonoual en que estaban los cuatro Tutulxiu al poniente de Zuina; el pais de donde vinieron fué Tulapan.

Translation of Brasseur.

C' est ici la série des epoques écoulées depuis que s' enfuirent les quatre Tutul Xiu de la maison de Nonoual etant a l'ouest de Zuinà, et vinrent de la terre de Tulapan.

Free translation suggested.

This is the order of the Katuns since the four Katuns during which the Tutulxiu left their home and country Nonoual to the west of Zuiua, and went from the land and city of Tula, having agreed together to this effect.

I have said nothing of the proper names in this paragraph. They are remarkable for the fact that three out of the four are unquestionably Nahuatl or Aztec, and hence they have given occasion for considerable theorizing in favor of the "Toltec" origin of the Maya civilization, and also of the Nahuatl descent of the princely family of the Tutulxiu.

Their name is the only one in the paragraph with a distinctively Maya physiognomy. It is a compound of *xiu*, the generic term for herb or plant, and *tutul*, a reduplicated form of *tul*, an abundance, an excess, as in the verb *tutulancil*, to overflow, etc. (*Diccionario de Ticul*, MS.). It would appear therefore to be a local name, and to signify a place where there was an abundance of herbage. The surname is Xiu only, and as such is still in use in Yucatan.

But it may also be claimed that even this is a Nahuatl name ; for also in that tongue *xiuitl* means a plant, as well as a turquoise, a comet, a year, and in composition a greenish or bluish color ; while *tototl* is a bird or fowl. The Maya *xiu* and the Nahuatl *xiuitl* (in which *itl* is a termination lost in composition) are undoubtedly the same word. Which nation borrowed it from the other? It is certainly a loan-word, for these two languages have no common origin, while, as we might expect from neighbors, each does have a number of loan-words from the other.

I answer that the Maya *xiu* is unquestionably a loan from the Nahuatl, and my reason for the opinion is that while in Maya the root *xiu* is sterile and has no relations to other words (unless perhaps to *xiitil*, to open like a flower, to brood as a bird, to augment, to grow), in Nahuatl it is a very fertile root, and nearly thirty compounds of it can be found in the dictionaries (See Molina, *Vocabulario de la Lengua Mexicana*,

fol. 159, verso). But the composition of the name follows
the Maya and not the Nahuatl analogy.

That in either language the name Tutulxiu can be translated "Bird-tree" (Vogelbaum), as is argued by Dr. Carl
Schultz-Sellack (*Archiv für Ethnologie*, Band XI, 1879), and
on which translation he bases a long argument, is very doubtful. It certainly could not in Maya; and in Nahuatl, *tototl*
in composition would drop both its terminal consonants.

The remaining names, Nonoual, Zuiua, Tula-pan, clearly
indicate their Nahuatl origin. Zuiua, which was erroneously
printed in Pio Perez's version as Zuina is Zuiva; Nonoual is
Nonohual; Tulapan, literally "the standard of Tula," refers
to the famous city of the Toltecs, presided over by Quetzalcoatl. All these names are borrowed directly from the myth
of this hero-god.

Zuiven was the name of the uppermost heaven, the abode
of the Creator Hometeuctli, the father of Quetzalcoatl, and
the place of his first birth as a divinity. In later days, when
the Quetzalcoatl myth had extended to the Kiches and
Cakchiquels, members of the Maya family in Guatemala,
"Tulan Zuiva" was identified with the Aztec Chicomoztoc,
the famous "Seven Caves," "Seven Ravines," or "Seven
Cities," from which so many tribes of Mexico, wholly diverse
in language and lineage, claimed that their ancestors emerged
in some remote past (compare the *Codex Vaticanus*, Lam. I;
Codex Zumarraga, chap. I, with the *Popol Vuh*, pp. 214, 227).
To this spot the ancestors of the Guatemalan tribes were
reported to have gone to receive their gods; from it issued
the Aztec god Huitzilopochtli; in it still were supposed to
dwell his mother and other mighty divinities; and Quetzalcoatl was again the youngest born of Iztac Mixcohuatl, the

mighty lord of the Seven Caves (Motolinia, *Historia de los Indios de Nueva España* p 10, etc.).

Tula, properly *Tollan*, a syncopated form of *Tonatlan*, which means "the place of the Sun," was a name applied to a number of towns in Mexico, all named after that magnificent city inhabited by the Tolteca ("dwellers in the place of the Sun"), servants and messengers of the Light-God their ruler, the benign, the virgin-born Quetzalcoatl. The common tradition ran that it was destroyed by the wiles of Tezcatlipoca, the brother, yet the eternal enemy, of Quetzalcoatl, and that at its destruction the Toltecs disappeared, no one knew whither, while Quetzalcoatl, after reigning a score of years in Cholula, journeyed far eastward to the home of the Sun, where he enjoyed everlasting life.

Nonohual also had a place in this myth. It was a mountain over against Tulan. There it was that the eldest sister of Quetzalcoatl resided. When he was made drunken by the insidious beverage handed him as a healing draught by Tezcatlipoca, he sent for this sister, held to her lips the intoxicating cup, and with her passed a night of debauch, the memory of which filled him with such shame that nevermore dared he face his subjects. Such is the story recited at length in the Aztec chronicle called the *Codex Chimalpopoca*.

Nonoalco was also the name of a small village near the city of Mexico which still appears on the maps. Sahagun tells us that some extreme eastern tribes in Mexico called themselves *Nonoalca* (*Historia de la Nueva España*, Lib. X, cap, XXIX, p 12); and the licenciate Diego Garcia de Palacio mentions "quatro lugares de Indios que llaman los Nunualcos" as dwelling, in his time (1576), in the eastern part of the province of San Salvador, of Aztec descent, and who had recently

come there. (*Carta al Rey de España*, p. 60, New York, 1860).
It should be mentioned in reference to these names and all
others of similar vocalization, that both in Maya and Nahuatl
the Spanish constantly confound the short ŏ and ŭ. As the
Bachelor Don Antonio Vasquez Gastelu observes: "usan de
la *o* algunos tan obscuramente, que tira algo à la pronuncia-
cion de la *u* vocal" (*Arte de lengua Mexicana*, fol. 1, verso,
La Puebla de los Angeles, 1726).

Señor Alfredo Chavero, in his Appendix to Duran's *Historia
de las Indias de Nueva España* (p. 45, Mexico, 1880), claims
that *Nonoalca* was the name given to the Maya-Kiche
tribes, or rather adopted by them, when, at an extremely
remote epoch, they penetrated to the central table land of
Mexico. He thinks that subsequently they became united
with the Toltecs, and were dispersed with that people at
the destruction of the city of Tula. The grounds for this
theory he claims to find in certain unpublished manuscripts, which unfortunately he does not give in extracts,
but only in general statements. Like much that this
writer presents, these assertions lack support. All the
names he quotes as of Nonoalca, that is, Maya origin, are
distinctly not of the latter tongue, but are Nahuatl. And the
introduction of the mystical city of Tula is of itself enough to
invest the story with the garb of unreality.

It is, in fact, nowhere in terrestrial geography that we need
look for the site of the Tula of Quetzalcoatl, nor at any time
in human history did the Tolteca ply their skillful hands, nor
Tezcatlipoca spread his snares to destroy them. All this is
but a mythical conception of the daily struggle of light and dark-
ness, and those writers who seek in the Toltecs the ancestors or
instructors of any nation whatsoever, make the once common

error of mistaking myth for history, fancy for fact. Therefore, any notion that Yucatan was civilized by the Toltecs
after their dispersion, or owes anything to them, as so many,
and I might say almost all recent writers have maintained, is
to me an absurdity.

This reference to the Quetzalcoatl myth at the commencement of the Maya chronicle needs not surprise us. We
encounter it also in the Kiche *Popol Vuh* and the Cakchiquel
Memorial de Tecpan Atitlan. These members of the Maya
family also grafted that myth upon their own traditions. As
history, it is valueless; but as indicative of a long and early
intercourse between the Maya and Nahuatl speaking tribes,
it is of great interest. As this question will also recur in
reference to various later passages in the Maya chronicles, I
will discuss it here.

One of the earliest historians of Yucatan, the Doctor Don
Pedro Sanchez de Aguilar, states that six hundred years before
the Spanish conquest the Mayas were vassals of the Aztecs,
and that they were taught or forced by these to construct the
extraordinary edifices in their country, such as are found at
Uxmal and Chichen Itza. His words are: "Fueron tan
politicos y justiciosos en Yucatan como los Mexicanos, cuyos
vasallos habian sido seis cientos años antes de la llegada de
los Españoles. De lo cual tan solamente hay tradicion y
memoria entre ellos por los famosos, grandes y espantosos
edificios de cal y canto y silleria y figuras y estatuas de piedra
labrada que dejaron en Oxumual [Uxmal] y en Chicheniza
que hoy se veen y se pudieran habitar." *Informe contra
Idolum Cultores del Obispado de Yucatan*, fol. 87 (Madrid,
1639).

The vague tradition here referred to was made part of the

testimony in a lawsuit at Valladolid, Yucatan, in 1618. These old documents were brought to light by the late eminent Yucatecan historian Doctor Justo Sierra, and Dr. Berendt took a copy in manuscript of the most important points. I think it worth while to insert and translate this testimony.

Villa de Valladolid—Año de 1618.

" Documento 1°. A la primera pregunta dijo este testigo que conoce al dicho Don Juan Kahuil y à la dicha Doña Maria Quen su legitima muger y que todos los contenidos en la pregunta, tuvo noticia muy larga de su padre de este testigo, porque fue en su antiguedad *ahkin,* sacerdote entre los naturales antiguos, antes que recibiesen agua de bautismo, como los susodichos contenidos en la pregunta vinieron del reino de Mexico y poblaron estas provincias, y que era gente belli- cosa y valerosa y Señores, y asi poblaron à Chichenica los unos, y otros se fueron hacia el Sur que poblaron á Bacalar, y hacia el Norte que poblaron la costa ; porque eran tres ò cuatro Señores y uno que se llamo *Tumispolchicbul* era deudo de Moctezuma, rey que fuè de los reinos de Mexico, y que *Cuhuikakcamalcacalpuc* era deudo muy cercano de dicho Don Juan Kahuil por parte de sus padres, y que dicha *Ixnahaucu- pul* hija de *Kukumcupul* fue muger de su abuelo de dicho D. Juan Kahuil, todos los cuales fueron los que vinieron de Mexico à poblar estas Provincias, gente principal y Señores, pues poblaron y se señorearon de esta tierra, porque como dicho tiene, le oyó decir al dicho su padre que eran tenidos, obedecidos y respetados como à Señores de esta tierra, y de uno de ellos procede el dicho D. Juan Kahuil, y de estos hay mucha noticia y dicho su padre le dijo muchas veces, que habia constancia entre ellos de lo sucedido por estos Señores.

" 2º. A la segunda pregunta dice este testigo, que como dicho tiene, oyó decir à su padre y otros Indios principales que los susodichos contenidos en la primera pregunta vinieron de los reynos de Mejico à poblar estàs provincias, los unos se quedaron en Chichinica que fueron los que edificaron los edificios sontuosos que hay en el dicho asiento, y otros se fueron à poblar à Bacalar, y otros fueron à poblar la costa hacia el norte, y este que fué à poblar la costa, se llamaba *Cacalpuc*, de donde procede el dicho D. Juan Kahuil, y estos que así se repartieron, fueron à poblar las provincias susodichas, y las tuvieron sugetas y en govierno, y que le cupo à un Cocom, el poblar en Chichinica, y le obedecian todos por Señor, y los de la isla de cuzumel le eran sugetos; y de allí (de Chicinica) se pasaron à la provincia de Sotuta, donde estaban, cuando los conquistadores vinieron, y siempre fueron tenidos, obedecidos y respetados como Señores.

" 3º. A la primera pregunta dijò este testigo que conoce al dicho D. Juan Kahuil, y à la dicha Da Maria Quen, su muger, y que de todos los contenidos en la pregunta, tuvo muy larga noticia de ellos, porque D. Juan Camal, cacique è gobernador que fuè del pueblo de Sisal, de los primeros que lo gobernaron por comision e titulo que lè diò el Oidor Tomas Lopez, oiendo como era de los antiguos caciques del dicho pueblo en estas provincias, lo trataba en conversacion à sus principales y este testigo, que siempre estaba en su casa, y fué alguacil mayor ordinario en ella, como los contenidos habian venido de Mejico à poblar esta tierra de Yucatan, y que los unos poblaron à Chichinica y hicieron los edificiós que estan en dicho asiento muy suntuosos, y que habiendo sido los que

vinieron de Mejico, cuatro deudos ò parientes con sus alle-
gados y gente que trajaron ; el uno pobló como dicho tiene
à Chichinica, y el otro fué à poblar à Bacalar, y el otro hacia
el Norte y pobló en la costa, y el otro fué hacia Cozumel ; è
poblaron con gente, y fueron Señores de estas provincias, y
las gobernaron y señorearon muchos años ; y que oyó decir
que uno de ellos llamado *Tanupolchicbul* era pariente de
Moctezuma, rey de Mejico.''

(*Translation.*)

CORPORATION OF VALLADOLID—YEAR 1618.

'' DOCUMENT No. 1. To the first question the witness answered that he knows the said Don Juan Kahuil and the said
Dona Maria Quen his lawful wife, and all those referred to in
the question; that this witness had full information from his
father, who formerly was *ahkin* or priest among the natives,
before they had received the water of baptism, how the parties above mentioned in the question came from the kingdom
of Mexico, and established towns[1] in these provinces, and
that they were a warlike and valiant people and lords, and
thus some of them established themselves at Chichen Itza,
and others went to the south and established towns at Bacalar, and toward the north and established towns on the coast ;
because they were three or four lords, and one, who was
named *Tumispolchicbul*, was a kinsman of Montezuma, king
of the kingdom of Mexico, and that *Cuhuikakcamalcacalpuc*
was a very near kinsman of the said Don Juan Kahuil on his
father's side, and that the said *Ixnahaucupul*, daughter of
Kukumcupul was wife of the grandfather of the said Don Juan

---

[1] The Spanish word '' poblar '' does not mean to people an uninhabited
country, but to found villages and gather the people into communities.

Kahuil, all of whom were those who came from Mexico to found towns in these provinces, prominent people and lords; then they founded towns and ruled this land, because as he said, he heard his said father say that they were regarded, obeyed and respected as lords of this land, and that from one of them proceeded the said Don Juan Kahuil; and of these there is abundant information, and his said father often said to him that there was unanimity among them as to what took place by these lords.

" 2ND. To the second question this witness answered that as he has said, he heard his father and other leading Indians say that the parties above mentioned in the first question came from the Kingdom of Mexico to found towns in these provinces; some remained in Chichen Itza, who were those who built the sumptuous edifices which are in the said locality; others went to found towns at Bacalar, and others to found towns on the coast to the north; and he who went to found towns on the coast was named Cacalpuc, from whom proceeds the said Don Juan Kahuil and those who thus made division went to found towns in the above mentioned provinces, and held them under subjection and government; and he chose a certain Cocom to rule in Chichen Itza, and they all obeyed him as lord, and those of the island of Cozumel were subject to him; and from there (from Chichen Itza) they passed to the province of Zotuta, where they were when the conquerors came, and they were always regarded, obeyed and respected as lords.

"3RD. To the first question this witness answered that he knew all the parties mentioned in the question and had abundant information about them, because Don Juan Camal who was chief and governor of Sisal, one of the first

who governed it by commission and brief given him by the
Auditor Tomas Lopez, being one of the ancient chiefs of the
said town in these provinces, spoke of the subject in conversation with his leading men and with this witness, who
was constantly in his house and was chief clerk in ordinary in
it, saying the parties mentioned had come from Mexico to
found towns in this land of Yucatan, and that some settled at
Chichen Itza, and erected the very stately edifices which are
in the said locality, and that those who came from Mexico
were four kinsmen or relatives with their friends and the people they brought with them; one settled as heretofore said at
Chichen Itza, one went to settle at Bacalar, one went toward
the north and settled on the coast, and the other went toward
Cozumel; and they founded towns with their people, and
were lords of these provinces, and governed them and ruled
them many years; and that he had heard it said that one of
them named *Tanupolchicbul* was a kinsman of Moctezuma,
King of Mexico."

This legend is also related, with some variation, by Herrera,
and as I shall have occasion more than once to refer to his
account, I shall translate it.

"At Chichen Itza, ten leagues from Itzamal, the ancients
say there reigned three lords, brothers, who came from the
west, and gathered together many people, and reigned some
years in peace and justice; and they constructed large and
very beautiful edifices. It is said that they lived unmarried
and very chastely; and it is added that in time one of them
was missing, and that his absence worked such bad results
that the other two began to be unchaste and partial; and thus
the people came to hate them, and slew them, and scattered

abroad, and deserted the edifices, especially the most stately one, which is ten leagues from the sea.

"Those who established themselves at Chichen Itza call themselves Itzas; among these there is a tradition that there ruled 'a great lord called Cuculcàn, and all agree that he came from the west; and the only difference among them is as to whether he came before or after or with the Itzas; but the name of the building at Chichen Itza, and what happened after the death of the lords above mentioned, show that Cuculcan ruled the country jointly with them.   He was a man of good disposition, was said not to have had either wife or children, and not to have known woman; he was devoted to the interests of the people, and for this reason was regarded as a god.   In order to pacify the land he agreed to found another city, where all business could be transacted.   He selected for this purpose a site eight leagues further inland from where now stands the city of Merida, and fifteen leagues from the sea.   There they erected a circular wall of dry stone, about a half quarter of a league in diameter, leaving in it only two gateways.   They erected temples, giving to the largest the name Cuculcàn, and also constructed around the wall the houses of the lords among whom Cuculcàn had divided the land, giving and assigning towns to each.   To the city he gave the name Mayapan, which means "the Standard of the Maya," as Maya is the name of their language.

"By this means the country was quieted and they lived in peace for some years under Cuculcan, who governed with justice, until, having arranged for his departure, and recommending them to continue the wise rule he had established, he left them and returned to Mexico by the same route he had come, remaining in Champoton some time, where, in memory of his journey, he erected a building in the sea, which remains to this day."[1]

Bishop Landa and some other early writers also give versions of this tradition, but do not add any facts to those in the above quotations. Evidently it was a widespread legend of the origin of the great buildings of Chichen Itza. Is it a tradition of fact or is it a myth?

I confess that to me it has a suspiciously mythical aspect. It is too similar to what I may call the standard hero-myth of the American Aborigines. Everywhere, both in North and South America, we find the myth of the four brothers who divided the land between them, one of whom is superior to the others and becomes the ruler and instructor of the ancestors of the nation. He does not die, but disappears, or goes to heaven, and is often expected to return. Just so in one of the Maya myths, Cuculcan did not return to Mexico, but rose to heaven, whence once every year he descended to his temple at Mayapan and received the gifts which from far and wide pious pilgrims had brought to his shrine (Landa, *Relacion*, p. 302). All these myths relate to the worship of the four cardinal points and to the Light-God, as I have shown in a previous work (*The Myths of the New World*, chap. III. New York, 1876).

The proper names in the legend have nothing of a Nahuatl appearance. They are all pure Maya. The "kinsman of Moctezuma," the second reading of whose name is the correct one, is given as *tan u pol chicbul*, "in front of the head of the jay-bird," the *chicbul* being what the Spaniards call the

---

[1] *Historia de las Indias Occidentales Dec.* IV, Lib. X, cap. II.

mingo rey, which I believe is a jay (Beltran, *Arte del Idioma Maya*, p. 229). The other long name is a compound of *Zuhuy kak camal cacal puc*. The historian Cogolludo informs us that *Zuhuy Kak*, literally " virgin fire," was the daughter of a king, afterwards deified as goddess of female infants (*Historia de Yucatan*, Lib. IV, cap. VIII). *Camal* was and is a common patronymic in Yucatan ; *cacalpuc* means " mountain land,"[1] and thus the whole name is easily identified as Maya. Possibly the member of the family Camal who bore the name was a priest of the goddess.

It will be noticed that neither the legend nor the legal testimony speaks of these foreigners as of a different language or lineage, but leaves us to infer the contrary. Had they been of Aztec race it would certainly have been noticed, for the Mayas had frequent mercantile relations with these powerful neighbors, they borrowed many words from the Nahuatl tongue, and single chiefs in Yucatan formed alliances with the Aztec rulers, and introduced Aztec warriors even into Mayapan, as is shown by the Chronicles I publish in this work, and also by the fact that a small colony of Aztecs, descendants of these mercenaries, was living in the province of Canul, west of Merida, when the Spaniards conquered the country (Landa, *Relacion*, p. 54). Therefore the Aztecs were no strangers to the Mayas, and doubtless the learned members of the priesthood and nobles in the fifteenth century were quite well aware of the existence of the powerful empire of Anahuac.

But regarding the legend I have quoted as, in part at least,

[1] *Cacal* is reduplicated from *cab*, land, province, town. The change from *b* to *l* is also seen in *cacalluum*, "tierra buena para sembrar," *Diccionario de Motul ;* also in the town names Tixcacal, Xcacal, etc.

I

based on actual history, we may accept the fact that there was an important emigration from Mexico, and yet not one of either Aztecs or "Toltecs." It must be remembered that the Huastecas, an important branch of the Maya family, occupied from time immemorial the coast of the Mexican Gulf north of Vera Cruz, and west to the mountains of Meztitlan, a province inhabited by a Nahuatl speaking race, but not subject to the dynasty of the Montezumas.

I have already referred briefly to their history, and it is possible that after their serious reverses, about 1450, they sent migratory bodies to their relatives in Yucatan. At any rate, there seems a consensus of testimony that the general trend of migration of the Maya race, was from north to south, and in Central America, from west to east.

We have in this paragraph examples of the use of three of the " numeral particles." *Cante bin ti katun*, literally, " it (*i. e.* time) went on for four katuns," and a few lines later *hunpel haab*, one year, *hunpiztun*, the first year.

The correct translation of *peten* has been debated; it is from the root *pet*, anything round, a circle, and usually means "island." By a later use it signifies any locality with definite boundaries, hence a province, or kingdom. The following is the entry in the *Diccionario de Motul :*

" PETEN ; isla, *item* provincia, region, comarca—*uay tu petenil Yucatan*, aqui en la provincia de Yucatan."

The name of the first leader, Holon Chan Tepeuh, does not recur in the Annals. Its signification is : *holon*, a generic name for large bees and flies ; *chan*, sufficient, powerful, still in use in Yucatan as a surname ; *tepeuh*, ruler, from *tepeual*, to rule. This last word is marked in the *Diccionario de Motul* as a "vocablo antiquo." It is of Aztec origin, as in the

Nahuatl language *tepeuani* means "conqueror." The name we are considering should probably be rendered "Holon Chan, the ruler." The province ruled by the Chan family at the time of the conquest was on the eastern coast, south of that of the Cupuls.

The name *Chacnouitan* is elsewhere, as we shall see, spelled *Chacnovitan* and *Chacnabiton.* I am inclined to believe the last mentioned is nearest the correct form. By Pio Perez it was supposed to be an ancient name of Yucatan, and he translates the phrase, *uay ti petene Chacnouitan,* by "à esta isla de Chacnavitan (Yucatan)." Dr. Valentini says : "the translation could as well stand for 'that distant island,'" and that "Chacnouitan was neither the whole nor the northern part of Yucatan, but a district situated in the southwest of the peninsula," (*loc. cit.* p. 38).

With this I cannot agree, as the adverb *uay* always refers to the place (in no matter how wide an accepation) where the speaker is. Therefore I translate it "here, (*i. e.* to this general country of Yucatan, and at first) to the province Chacnouitan." The province referred to was, I doubt not, somewhere around Lake Peten. The word *chac* is often used in local names in Yucatan, and usually means either "water" or "red," as it is a homonym with several significations.

Several names similar to it are found in the Peten district. On Lake Yaxta, are the ruins of the very ancient city Napeten, and that lake may have once been called "Chac-napeten," "the water of Napeten." Again, on the road from Peten to Bacalar is the town Chacnabil, and the compound *Chacnabiltan* would mean "toward or in the direction of Chacnabil" (see *Itinerarios y Leguarios que proceden de Merida, etc.,* p. 15, Merida, 1851). The Itzas always remembered the

Peten district, and when they met with reverses in northern Yucatan, they returned to it and established an important State there, which was not destroyed until the last decade of the seventeenth century.

3. *Hunpel haab minan ti hokal haab*, "one year lacking from five score years."

The name Ahmekat is probably an old form for *ahmeknah* or *ahmektan*, both of which are given in the *Diccionario de Motul* for chieftain, leader, captain.

4. *Lai tun*, the relative *lai* with the particle *tun*, which is called by Beltran a "particula adornativa." *uchci* is the aorist of the defective verb *uchul, uchi, uchuc*, to happen, to take place, come to pass. *Emob* is the third plural of *emel*, to descend, to disembark, arrive. Pio Perez translates the phrase *ca emob uay lae*, "luego bajaron aqui." As this was written in the province of Mani, the "here" now refers in a narrower sense to the vicinity of the writer. The word *chuulte* I take to be an error of transcription for *uchci*, as it is so translated by Pio Perez. It is noteworthy that the word *chicpahci*, "discovered," conveys the sense that Chichen Itza was already in existence when the migration here recorded reached northen Yucatan. It is from *chicul*, a sign or mark by which something is recognized.

Of the proper names in this section Bakhalal, "the cane-brakes" (*halal*, the cane, *bak*, a roll or enclosure), is the modern province of Bacalar, on the east coast of the peninsula. *Ziyan caan* appears to be used as a synonym of it, or else refers to a part of it. Its meaning is a picturesque reference to the view from the sea shore, where the horizon is clearly defined, and the sky seems to rise from the water, "the birth of the sky;" *Ziyan*, birth, *caan*, sky.

The name Chi Cheen Itza was that of one of the grandest ancient cities of Yucatan. *Cheen* is the name applied to a tract of low-lying fertile land, especially suitable to the production of cacao (Berendt); *chi* is edge or border. It is therefore a name referring to a locality , " on the border of the *cheen* of the Itzas." *Cheen* also means well or cistern, and another derivation is " at the mouth of the well," as *chi* can also be rendered " mouth;" either of these is appropriate to the features of the locality, as it is a fertile low-lying tract with two large natural reservoirs near by.

5. *Paxi*, from *paaxal*, a neuter form of the active verb *pa*, to break in pieces ; it means " to go to pieces, to fall in ruins, to be depopulated or deserted." Applied to a city it is often translated " to be destroyed," but it does not convey quite so positive a meaning. *Kuyan uincob*, " men of God," from *Ku* the general name for Divinity. Chichen Itza was one of the chief centres of religious life in Yucatan, and its priests were esteemed among the most learned in the peninsula.

The name Chanputun, Champoton, or, reversed, Potonchan, is derived by Gomara from the Nahuatl *potonia*, to smell badly, and *chan*, house (in composition). Elsewhere, however, we find it in the form Chakanputun, and this is Maya. *Chakan* is the term applied to a grassy plain, a savanna, and it was especially applied to the ancient province in which the city of Ho, now Merida, was situated, as appears from the following entry in the *Diccionario de Motul, MS.*

"AHCHAKAN: el que es de Mérida, o de los pueblos de aquella comarca, que se llama *Chakan*."

The correct form of the name is probably *Chakan peten*, the savanna region.

6. The only obscure expression in this section is *yalan che*,

yalan aban, yalan ak. This often recurs in the ancient Maya manuscripts, and was evidently a well-known formula, probably the refrain of one of their ancient chants. In Mr. Stephens' translation it is rendered "under the uninhabited mountains" (!) which is an attempt to render Pio Perez's words " bajo los montes despoblados," "in the uninhabited forests." *Aban* or *haban* is an obsolete word, only found in compounds, as *yoxhaban*, huts made of branches. Both it and *ak* were the names of various branches or twigs. The phrase is literally " under the trees, under the branches, under the foliage," and meant that those who thus lived were homeless and houseless. It is a striking testimony to the love of solid buildings and walled cities which .characterized the Mayas.

I will add a verse from a curious prophetic chant in one of the Books of Chilan Balam, where this expression occurs, and which is an interesting example of these strange songs.

TZOLAH TI AHKIN CHILAM.

(Recital of the priest Chilam.)

Uien, uien, a man uah ;
Uken, uken, a man haa ;
Tu kin, puz lum pach,
Tu kin, tzuch lum ich,
Tu kin, naclah muyal,
Tu kin, naclah uitz,
Tu kin, chuc lum ɔiic,
Tu kin, hubulhub,
Tu kin, coɔ yol chelem,
Tu kin, eɔeleɔ,
Tu kin, ox ɔalab u nak yaxche,

Tu kin, ox chuilab xotem,

Tu kin, pan tzintzin

Yetel banhob yalan che yalan haban.

Translation.

Eat, eat, thou hast bread ;

Drink, drink, thou hast water ;

On that day, dust possesses the earth,

On that day, a blight is on the face of the earth,

On that day, a cloud rises,

On that day, a mountain rises,

On that day, a strong man seizes the land,

On that day, things fall to ruin,

On that day, the tender leaf is destroyed,

On that day, the dying eyes are closed,

On that day, three signs are on the tree,

On that day, three generations hang there,

On that day, the battle flag is raised,

And they are scattered afar in the forests.

7. *Heɔob*, from *heɔ*, *heɔel* or *eɔ*, to fix firmly, to settle, to found : *heɔel ca cah uaye*, let us settle here, '' poblamos aqui '' (*Dicc. de San Francisco*, MS.).

8. The founding of Uxmal by Ahcuitok Tutulxiu is recorded in this paragraph ; *ahcui* is the name of a species of owl , *tok* is the flint stone. By some old writers Uxmal is spelled Oxmal, which would give the meaning '' to pass thrice,'' *ox*, three, *mal*, to pass. From *mal*, preterite *mani*, also was derived the name of the chief city of the Tutulxiu, with a peculiar signification explained in a note on a previous page.

Mr. Stephens has taken considerable pains to prove that

Uxmal with its astonishing edifices was inhabited at and after the conquest (*Incidents of Travel in Yucatan*, Vol. II, p. 259); there may, indeed, have been an Indian village there, but the first European traveler who has left us a description of it, and who visited it in 1586, when many natives, born before the conquest, were still living, describes the massive buildings as even then in ruins, and very large trees growing upon them.   An old Indian told him that according to their traditions, these structures had at that time been built nine hundred years, and that their builders had left the country nearly that long ago.   (*Relacion Breve y Verdadera de algunas cosas de las muchas qui sucedieron al Padre Fray Alonzo Ponce*, in the *Coleccion de Documentos para la Historia de España*, vol. LVIII, p. 461.)

The phrase *u heɔicab Ahcuitok Tutulxiu Uxmal* is translated by Pio Perez "se pobló en Uxmal," established himself in Uxmal," conveying the impression that he merely moved to that city.   This is, however, not the sense of the original. *Heɔicab* is an active verb governing Uxmal as its direct object, and means to found firmly or promptly.

The expression *halach uinicil*, the real man, the true man, is a common idiom for governor or ruler, he being the only "real man" in an autocratic community (ante p. 26).

The name of Mayapan is given in the form Mayalpan, which I think is dialectic.   It is spoken of as an established city under the joint rule of several chiefs at the date of the founding of Uxmal.

9.   This paragraph describes how the ruler of the Itzas lost his share in the government of Mayapan.   *Kebanthan*, literally a plot, or to plot to do some injury—" concertar de hacer algun mal, y el tal concierto," *Diccionario de Motul*,

MS. I have followed Pio Perez in translating "against Hunac Eel," although "by Hunac Eel" seems more correct. Elsewhere the name is Hunac Ceel. Ancona argues that he was a member of the Cocom family (*Hist. de Yucatan*, I. p. 157).

Several of the names of the seven "men of Mayapan" have a Nahuatl appearance. Kakaltecat = Cacaltecatl, He of the Crow; Ytzcuat = Itzcoatl, Smirch-faced snake; Xuchueuet = Xochitl, the rose or flower; Pantemit = Pantenamitl, the Conqueror of the city wall. These would seem to bear out what Landa and Herrera say, to the effect that at one period the rulers of Mayapan invited Aztec warriors from the province of Tabasco to come and dwell in the city and aid them in controlling the inhabitants.

Both Dr. Valentini and Señor Pio Perez are of opinion the Katuns at the commencement of this paragraph should read the 10th, 8th and 6th, instead of the 11th, 9th and 6th, as it is necessary in order to establish consistency with what follows.

10. This is one of the most obscure sections in the chronicle. The phrase *tumenel u uahal uahob* is rendered by Pio Perez " because he made war," while Brasseur translates it " because of his great feasts." The meaning of the root *uah* is maize cakes, or, more generally, bread. The *Diccionario de Motul* gives: " UAHIL; banquete, convite ó comida," which is in favor of Brasseur's translation.

Oxlahun uuɔ, "thirteen divisions;" *uuɔ* or *uuuɔ* means literally a fold or double, and hence appears to have been applied to ranks of men in double rows. I do not find, however, any such meaning given in the dictionaries. As a numeral particle it is used to count whatever occurs in folds or doubles.

The number thirteen had a sacredness attached to it, from its frequent use in the calendar. It appears from a passage in the *Popol Vuh* that the Cakchiquels, Pokomams and Pokomchis also divided their tribes into thirteen sections (*Popol Vuh*, p. 206). In the Maya language, 13 is also used to signify a great but indefinite number: thus *oxlahun cacab*, thirteen generations, is equivalent to "forever"; *oxlahun pixan*, thirteen times happy, is to be happy in the supreme degree; more remote from customary analogies is the phrase for "full moon," *oxlhaun caan u*, literally "the thirteen-sky moon," the moon which fills with its light the whole sky (*Diccionario de Motul*, MS.).

The phrase *u ɔabal u natob* is not translated at all in the English rendering in Stephens' *Travels*, nor in that of Valentini. Brasseur paraphrases it "by him who gives intelligence."

The proper names Ulmil and Ulil seem both to be derived from *ula*, host, the master of the feast.

Here, again, I shall give the originals of the two previous translators.

Translation of Pio Perez.

"En este mismo periodo ô *katun* del 8° ahau fueron á destruir al rey Ulmil porque le hacia la guerra al rey de Izamal Ulil. Trece divisiones de combatientes tenia cuando los dispersó Hunac-eel para escarmentarlos: la guerra se concluyó en el 6° ahau á los 34 años."

Translation of Brasseur.

"C'est dans la même période du Huit Ahau qu 'ils allèrent attaquer le roi Ulmil, à cause de ses grands festins avec Ulil, roi d' Ytzmal: ils avaient treize divisions de troupes, lorsqu'ils furent défaits par Hunac-Eel, par celui qui donne l' intelligence. Au Six Ahau, c'en etait fait, après trente quatre ans."

The name Hunac Eel should be Hunac Ceel, as it is given in the other chronicles.   It means "he who causes great fear," *hunac* in composition means much, great, and *ceel*, cold, also the fright and terror which makes one shiver as with cold ("espanto, asombro ô turbacion que causa frio." *Dicc. de Motul*, MS).

11. This important section describes the destruction of the great city of Mayapan, which occurred somewhere between A.D. 1420–1450.   The reasons given for the act are not clear.

Tumenel u pach tulum, tumenel multepal ich cah Mayalpan, appears to me to have the precise meaning I have given in the text ; but Pio Perez translates the passage thus " fué invadido por los hombres de Itza y su rey Ulmil, el territorio fortificado de Mayalpan, porque tenia murallas, y porque gobernaba en comun el pueblo de aquella ciudad."

The expression *multepal*, from *mul*, to do an act jointly, or in common, and *tepal*, to govern, is interesting as showing that the government of the country in its golden days of prosperity was not one of an autocratic monarch, but a league or confederation of the principal chiefs of the peninsula.   This is also borne out by the descriptions of the ancient government to be found in the pages of Landa and Herrera.

The Itzas seized the territory in and around Mayapan, but they were not the ones who destroyed the city.   This was the work of *Ahuitzilbul*, foreign mountaineers.   *Ɔul*, is the common term for a foreigner in Maya, and is now-a-days applied especially to the whites.   *Uitz*, mountain, is used with reference to the high sierra which runs through central Yucatan, and so Pio Perez understood *ahuitzil*, "los que tenian sus ciudades en la parte montañosa."   This is probably correct, though

we do not know to whom this appellation refers.   Yet it may
be added that another meaning can be given to the phrase ;
uitz is the term applied by the natives in some parts of the
peninsula to the artificial mounds or pyramids on which their
temples were situated, which are usually called *muul*.[1]   In
this sense *ahuitzil ɔul* should be rendered " foreigners who
had great pyramids."

The words *tan cah Mayapan* (not Mayalpan as before) are
rendered by Pio Perez and Brasseur as the name of a province
or district; but as they simply mean " in the middle of the
city of Mayapan," it appears to be their signification here.

12. " After the fortress was depopulated " or destroyed.
This no doubt refers to the fortress of Mayapan, spoken of in
the previous section.   Aguilar and his companions were
wrecked on the coast of Yucatan, in 1511, and this is probably the earliest date of any actual landing of Europeans, although in 1506, Pinzon had sighted the eastern shores.

13. *Mayacimil*, " the death of the Mayas," a term applied
to a general and fatal pestilence.   Such are referred to by
Landa (*Relacion*, § X.) and Cogolludo (*Historia de Yucatan*,
Lib. IV, cap. VI),   The *Diccionario de Motul*, MS. has this
entry:

" MAYACIMIL : una mortandad grande que fué en Yucatan.
Y tomase por qualquier mortandad y pestilencia que lleva
mucha gente."

Noh kakil, noh, great, *kak*, fire, is the usual word for the
smallpox.

---

[1] "En toda la Peninsula existen unos cerros á mano ó monticulos arti-
ficiales, que comunmente llaman los naturales en idioma Maya *Muul* en
algunos lugares, y en otros *Uitz*."   Don Jose T. Cervera in the *Revista
de Merida*, Dec. 3, 1871.

The reference to the death of Ahpula, who, as we learn from another chronicle, was a member of the royal Xiu family, is especially valuable as assigning a definite date in both the Maya and European calendars. It is specified with great minuteness, and yet Pio Perez made the serious error in his computations regarding the Maya calendar of reading "the sixth year of the 13th ahau" instead of "six years from the close of the 13th ahau," as, in fact, he himself elsewhere translated it.

The expression *u xocol haab ti lakin cuchie*, "the reckoning of the year was toward the East," refers to the circle or wheel marked with the four cardinal points by which the years were arranged with reference to the four "year-bearers" Kan, Muluc, Ix and Cauac.

The last words of this section, "sixty years after the fortress was destroyed," are an obvious error, as in the preceding section this date is said to be that of the first arrival of the Spaniards.

14. *Kul uincob*, "mighty men," from *kul*, strong, powerful, probably akin to *ku*, god, but not with the religious signification which *kuyen* has (see page 125). *Caputzihil*, literally "to be born a second time." Bishop Landa assures us positively that a rite of baptism was known to the Mayas before the arrival of the whites, and that this name was applied to it (*Relacion*, p. 144). As will be seen on a later page, Maya writers usually employed another term to express Christian baptism.

The year in which Bishop Francisco Toral first came to Yucatan was 1562 (Cogolludo, *Hist. de Yucatan*, Lib. VI, cap. VI). He died in Mexico in 1571.

The remainder of this chronicle has never been translated or published. It refers to facts after the Conquest, but I think it of interest to give it completely, as its manner of dealing with known dates will throw light on its general accuracy.

15. Bishop Diego de Landa, second bishop of the diocese of Merida, died at that city in 1579, aged fifty-four years. The first missionaries that came to Mani were Fathers Villalpando and Benavente, in 1547 (Cogolludo, *Hist.*, Lib. V, cap. VII). The convent there was established in 1549.

16. No town of the name Yokhaa is now known. But I find on the ancient native map of Mani, dating from 1557, given by Stephens (*Travels in Yucatan*, Vol. II, p. 264), a locality marked *Yokha*, marked with a cross. This is no doubt the reference in the text.

17. The Auditor Don Tŏmas Lopez came to Yucatan from Guatemala. He was in Yucatan as early as 1552, and published laws in that year (Cogolludo, Lib. V, cap. XIX, Lib. VII, cap. XI). A hospital was founded very early in Mani, according to Cogolludo, but he does not give the exact date (*ibid.*, Lib. IV, cap. XX).

18. Doctor Don Diego Quijada arrived in Yucatan in 1562, and remained until 1565.

19. When Landa was provincial, 1562–65, various Indians were hanged on account of the prevalence of suicide.

20. What Marshall is referred to is uncertain, *thulub* should probably be *chulub*, and so I have translated it. Berendt suggested *ca botab chulub*, "when they paid for water," the reference being to a great drought.

21. An epidemic of measles and smallpox, in 1609, is referred to by Cogolludo (Lib. IX, cap. I).

22. In 1610 three Indians of Tekax were hanged for having killed their chief Don Pedro Xiu (Cogolludo, Lib. IX, cap. I).

23. The reference is to a census or assessment of the town. None is mentioned in this year by Cogolludo, nor does he speak of the Judge Diego Pareja.

From the Book of Chilan Balam of Tizimin.

———

Tizimin is a town of some importance, in the district of Valladolid, about a hundred miles east of Merida. The "Book of Chilan Balam" which was found there is one of the most ancient known, and appears to have been written about the close of the sixteenth century. It is now in the possession of the eminent antiquary, the Canon Crescencio Carrillo y Ancona, of Merida, who has described it in his work on Maya literature.[1] It contains 26 leaves, without numeration, and on the 17th this chronicle is inserted without title or prefatory remarks. It is evidently a version of that previously given from the Book of Mani, although a few additional particulars are stated, and there seems to have been an attempt to arrange the epochs in more completeness.

This has led to the insertion of a number of katuns which I think it evident do not properly come into the count. To correct the list the ka-

[1] *Disertacion sobre la Historia de la Lengua Maya ò Yucateca,* in the *Revista de Merida,* 1870, p. 128.

tuns 8th, 6th, and 4th, mentioned in §2, should be considered the same as 8th, 6th, and 4th, repeated in §3 and §4.   Again, in section 11, the 8th katun, on which the attack on Mayapan occurs, is to be considered the same as the 8th with which §12 begins, and the whole of the 25 katuns which are either stated to have intervened, or must be added in order to make the series correct, are to be omitted.   Finally, the 8th katun at the close of §10 should immediately follow the 10th at the close of §8.

1. Uaxac ahau.

   Uac ahau

   Can ahau.

   Cabil ahau—[1] cakal hab catac humppel hab tu humpiztun ahoxlahunahau.

2. Oxlahun ahau.

   Uaxac ahau.

   Uac ahau.

   Ca ahau ; kuchci chacnabiton mekat tutul xiu, humppel hab mati hokal hab.

3. Uaxac ahau ; uch cuchi [2] canpahal chicħen Ytza ; uch cu chicpahal tzucubte Zian can lae.

4. Can ahau.

   Cabil ahau.

   Oxlahun ahau ; lai tzolci pop.

5. Buluc ahau.

   Bolon ahau.

   Uuc ahau.

   Ho ahau.

[1] cankal.   [2] canlaahal.

Ox ahau.

Hun ahau; lahunkal hab cu tepal chichen Ytza, ca paxi ca binob t cahtal chakanputun ti yanhi yotochob ahYtzaob kuyan uinicobi.

6. Uac ahau; chuccu lumil chakanputun.

Can ahau.

Cabil ahau.

Oxlahun ahau.

Buluc ahau.

Bolon ahau.

Uuc ahau.

Ho ahau.

Ox ahau.

Hun ahau.

Lahca ahau.

Lahun ahau.

Uaxac ahau; paxci chakanputun; oxlahun-kal hab cu tepal chacanputun tumen Ytza ¹unincob; ca talob u tzaclob yotochob tucaten; ca u zatahob be chakanputun; lay u katunil ²biciob ahYtzaob yalan che, yalan haban, yalan ak ti numyaob.

7. Vac ahau.

Can ahau; cakal hab ca talob u heɔ yotochob tu caten; ca u zatahob be chankanputun.

Cabil ahau.

¹ uinicob.   ² binciob.

Oxlahun ahau.

Buluc ahau.

Bolon ahau.

Vuc ahau.

Ho ahau.

Ox ahau.

Hun ahau.

Lahca ahau.

8. Lahun ahau; u heɔcicab ahzuitok tutulxiu
uxmal; lahunkal hab cuchi ca heɔiob lum
Uxmal.

9, 10. Buluc ahau.

Bolon ahau.

Uuc ahau.

Ho ahau.

Ox ahau.

Hun ahau.

Lahca ahau.

Lahun ahau.

Uaxac ahau; paxci u halach vinicil chichen
Ytza tu kebanthan hunac ceel, ah zinte yut
chan, tzumte cum, taxal, pantemit, xuchve-
vet, Itzcoat, kakal cat, lai u kaba u uinicilob
lae uuctulob tumen u uahal uahob y ytzmal
ulil ahau: oxlahun uuɔ u katunilob ca paxob
tumen hunac ceel, tumen u ɔabal u natob.

11. Uac ahau.

Can ahau; cakal hab ca chuci u lumil ahau, tumen u kebanthan hunac ceel.

Cabil ahau.

Oxlahun ahau.

Buluc ahau.

Bolon ahau.

Uuc ahau.

Ho ahau.

Ox ahau.

Hun ahau.

Lahca ahau.

Uaxac ahau; uchci puchtun ich paa Mayapan tumen u pach tulum, tu tumen multepal ich cah mayapan.

Uac ahau.

Cabil ahau; oxlahun tun mani ɔulob u yaxil cob u lumil Yucatan tzuˀᵘbte; cankal hab catac oxlahun pizi.

Buluc ahau.

Bolon ahau.

Uuc ahau.

Ho ahau.

Ox ahau.

Hun ahau.

Lahca ahau.

Lahun ahau,

Uaxac ahau.

Uac ahau.

Can ahau.

Cabil ahau.

Oxlahun ahau.

Buluc ahau.

12. Uaxac ahau; paxci cah mayapan tumenel
    vitzil ɔul ; lahunkal hab catac cankal habi.

13. Can ahau ; uchi maya cimlal ocnalkuchil
    ych paa.

    Cabil ahau ; uchci nohkakil.

    Oxlahun ahau; ¹uchci cimil ahpulha, uacppel
    hab u binel ca ɔococ u xol oxlahun ahau
    cuchie, ti yan u xocol hab ti lakin cuchie,
    canil kan, cumlahi pop hool han, tu holhun
    zip catac oxppeli, bolon imix u kinil cimci
    ahpulha laitun hab =1536 cuchi.

14. Buluc ahau ; ulci ɔulob——kul uincob ti la-
    kin u talob ca ulob uai tac lumile.

    Bolon ahau; hopci xptianoil; uchci caputzihil;
    lai li ichil u katunil ulci yax obispo toral
    heix hab cu ²xinbal cuchie—1544.

15. Vuc ahau; cimci obispo Landa ichil u katunil.

16. Ho ahau, ca yum cahi padre mani lai hab cu

¹ uchuc.   ² ximbal.

ximbal cuchi la—1550; lai hab cu ximbal
ca cahiob yok ha, 1552 cuchi.

17. 1559, hab ca uli oydor ca paki spital.

18. 1560, u habil ca uli Doctor quixada yax
halach uinic uai ti lume.

19. 1562, hab ca uchci chuitab.

20. 1563, hab ca uli mariscal.

21. 1569, hab ca uchi kakil.

22. 1619, u habil ca hichi u cal 'ahkaxob.

23. 1611, hab ca ɔibtabi cah tumenel Jues.

[1] tikaxob.

1. The eighth ahau.

   The sixth ahau.

   The fourth ahau.

   The second ahau; four score years and one year to the first year of the thirteenth ahau.

2. The thirteenth ahau.

   The eighth ahau.

   The sixth ahau.

   The fourth ahau; Mekat Tutulxiu arrived at Chacnabiton; five score years lacking one year.

3. The eighth ahau; it occurred that Chichen Itza was learned about; the discovery of the province of Zian can took place.

4. The fourth ahau.

   The second ahau.

   The thirteenth ahau; then Pop was counted in order.

5. The eleventh ahau.

   The ninth ahau.

   The seventh ahau.

   The fifth ahau.

The third ahau.

The first ahau; ten score years they ruled Chichen Itza, then it was destroyed and they went to live at Chakanputun, where were the houses of those of Itza, holy men.

6. The sixth ahau; the land of Chakanputun was seized.

The fourth ahau.

The second ahau.

The thirteenth ahau.

The eleventh ahau.

The ninth ahau.

The seventh ahau.

The fifth ahau.

The third ahau.

The first ahau.

The twelfth ahau.

The tenth ahau.

The eighth ahau; Chakanputun was abandoned; for thirteen score years Chakanputun was ruled by the men of Itza; then they came in search of their houses a second time; and they lost the road to Chakanputun; in this katun those of Itza were under the trees, under the boughs, under the branches, to their sorrow.

7. The sixth ahau.

The fourth ahau: two score years, and they came and established their houses a second time; when they lost the road to Chakanputun.

The second ahau.

The thirteenth ahau.

The eleventh ahau.

The ninth ahau.

The seventh ahau.

The fifth ahau.

The third ahau.

The first ahau.

The twelfth ahau.

8. The tenth ahau ; Ahzuitok Tutulxiu founded Uxmal: ten score years had passed when they established the territory of Uxmal.

9, 10. The eleventh ahau.

The ninth ahau.

The seventh ahau.

The fifth ahau.

The third ahau.

The first ahau.

The twelfth ahau.

The tenth ahau.

The eighth ahau ; the ruler deserted (depopulated) Chichen Itza, on account of the plot of Hunac Ceel; Ahzinteyut Chan, Tzumtecum, Taxal, Pantemit, Xuchueuet, Itzcoat, Kakalcat, these were the names of the seven men; on account of the banquet with Ulil, ruler of Itzmal; there were thirteen divisions of warriors when they were driven out by Hunac Ceel, in order that they might know what was to be given.

11. The sixth ahau.

The fourth ahau: two score years; then the ruler seized the land on account of the plot of Hunac Ceel.

The second ahau.

The thirteenth ahau.

The eleventh ahau.

The ninth ahau.

The seventh ahau.

The fifth ahau.

The third ahau.

The first ahau.

The twelfth ahau.

The tenth ahau.

The eighth ahau; fighting took place in the fortress Mayapan, on account of the seizure of the castle, and on account of the joint government in the city of Mayapan.

The sixth ahau.

The second ahau : on the thirteenth foreigners passed, they say for the first time,
to this land, the province Yucatan; four
score years and thirteen.'

The eleventh ahau.

The ninth ahau.

The seventh ahau.

The fifth ahau.

The third ahau.

The first ahau.

The twelfth ahau.

The tenth ahau.

The eighth ahau.

The sixth ahau.

The fourth ahau.

The second ahau.

The thirteenth ahau.

The eleventh ahau.

12. The eighth ahau; Mayapan was depopulated by foreigners from the mountains;
ten score years and four score years.

13. The fourth ahau; the pestilence, the general
death, took place in the fortress.

The second ahau; the smallpox took place.

The thirteenth ahau; the death of Ahpulha
took place; it was the sixth year when ended

the count of the thirteenth ahau; the count of
the year was from the east, (the month) Pop
passed on the fifth kan; on the eighteenth
of (the month) Zip, 9 Imix, was the day
Ahpulha died; it was the year 1536.

14. The eleventh ahau; foreigners arrived—
mighty men from the east; they came, they
arrived here in this land.

The ninth ahau; Christianity began; baptism
took place; also in this katun came the first
bishop Toral; the year which was passing
was—1544.

15. The seventh ahau; bishop Landa died in
this katun.

16. The fifth ahau; the Fathers settled at Mani;
the year that was passing was 1550; in the
year 1552 they settled upon the water.

17. 1559; this year came the auditor and built
the Hospital.

18. 1560; this year arrived Doctor Quixada,
the first governor here in this land.

19. 1562; this year took place the hanging.

20. 1563; this year came Mariscal.

21. 1569; this year smallpox occurred.

22. 1610; this year those of Tekax were hanged.

23. 1611; this year the towns were written down
by the Judge.

NOTES.

The entire omission of the introductory paragraph of the Mani chronicle, with its references to the Quetzalcoatl myth, is noteworthy.

As neither chronicle begins with the beginning of an Ahau Katun, it is obvious that some era was fixed upon in later days from which to count the Katuns backward in time to the dawn of tradition, as well as forward.

2. On the name *Chacnabiton* see page 123.

3. *Canpahal* I take to be an old form of *canchahal* or *can-laahal*, both of which mean to learn or learn about. On *Zian can* see page 124.

4. I am at a loss for the exact bearing of the expression *lai tzolci Pop*. Pop is the first month in the Maya year; *tzoolol* is "to be counted in order" (*Dicc. Motul*); the preterite in *ci* would seem to justify the rendering "since then Pop was counted in regular succession;" (see remarks on the effect of *ci*, on page 106); in other words, that the calendar was adopted at that time, which was also at the beginning of an Ahau Katun, and, by the count given (supplying the katuns not mentioned by the writer) thirty katuns, 600 years, since their traditions began.

6. *Chuccu*, passive of *chucah*, to seize, take possession of.

Zatahob be, "they lost the road," probably meant, in a figurative sense, that they were prevented by intervening unfriendly tribes from continuing their intercourse with the

150

western coast. *Biciob*, evidently for *binciob*. The expression *yalan che, yalan haban, yalan ak*, has already been explained (page 126).

13. *Ocnakuchil*. The derivation of this word is stated to be from *ocol*, to enter, *na*, the houses, *kuch*, the crow or buzzard, the number of the dead being so great that the carrion birds entered the dwellings to prey upon the bodies.

In the account of Ahpula's death *ca ɔococ* should, I think, read *ca ma ɔococ*, "when not yet was ended."

III. THE RECORD OF THE COUNT OF THE KATUNS.

From the Book of Chilan Balam of Chumayel.

The village of Chumayel is about six leagues east of Mani, and within the boundaries of the province anciently ruled by the Xiu family.

The copy of the Book of Chilan Balam which was found there was a redaction made by an Indian, Don Juan Josef Hoil, in 1782. Like all these volumes it is a sort of common place book, in which were copied miscellaneous articles from much older manuscripts. One of these bears the date 1689, but most of them have no date attached. Hoil's original is, I believe, in the possession of the Canon Crescencio Carrillo y Ancona, of Merida. A fac-simile copy, by the hand of the late Dr. Berendt, is in my possession.

At the close of the volume, ff. 40-44, are found three summaries of the ancient history of Yucatan, which are those I am about to give. They have never been translated from the original, nor published in any form, and they contain details of interest. They are evidently from different sources, and are also different from those previously given.

152

TEXT.

U kahlay u xocan katunob uchi u chictahal u Chicħeen Ytza uchi lae lay ɔiban ti cab lae uchebal yoheltabal tumen hijmac yolah yohel te ti xocol katun lae.

---

1.   VI. Uac ahau uchci u chictahal u chicħeen Ytza.

   IIII. Can ahau lae.

   II. Cabil ahau.

   XIII. Oxlahun ahau tzolci.pop.

   XI. Buluc ahau.

   IX. Bolon ahau.

   VII. Uuc ahau.

   V. Ho ahau.

   III. Ox ahau.

   I. Hun ahau.

   XII. Lahca ahau.

   X. Lahun ahau ; paxci u chicħeen Ytza ; uchi oxlahun uuɔ katun cacahi chakanputun ti yotochob u katunil.

2.   VI. Uac ahau.

  IIII. Can ahau; chucci u lumil tumenob Chakanputun.

  II. Cabil ahau.

  XIII. Oxlahun ahau.

  XI. Buluc ahau.

  IX. Bolon ahau.

  VII. Uuc ahau.

  V. Ho ahau.

  III. Ox ahau.

  I. Hun ahau.

  XII. Lahca ahau.

  X. Lahun ahau.

  VIII. Uaxac ahau; paxci chakan putunob tumenob ah Ytza uinicob ca taliob u tzacle u yotochob tu caten; oxlahun uuɔ u katunil; cahanob chakan putunob tic yotochob; layli u katunil binciob ah Ytzaob yalan che, yalan haban, yalan ak, ti numyaob lae.

3.   VI. Uac ahau.

  IIII. Can ahau.

  II. Cabil ahau.

  XIII. Oxlahun ahau.

  XI. Buluc ahau.

IX. Bolon ahau.

VII. Uuc ahau.

V. Ho ahau.

III. Ox ahau.

I. Hun ahau.

XII. Lahca ahau.

X. Lahun ahau.

VIII. Uaxac ahau; paxci ahYtza uinicob ti yotochob tu caten, tumen u keban-than hun nac ceel, tumen u uahal uahob *y* ahYtzmal; oxlahunuuɔ u katunil cahanobi ca paxiob tumen hun nac ceel, tumen a ɔabal u natob ahYtzaob lae.

4. VI. Uac ahau.

IIII. Can ahau: chucci u luumil ichpaa Mayapan tumen AhYtza uinicob, likulob ti yotoche tumenel ahYtz-malob, tumen u kebanthan - - - - hun nac ceel lae.

5. II. Cabil ahau.

XIII. Oxlahun ahau.

XI. Buluc ahau.

IX. Bolon ahau.

VII. Uuc ahau,

V. Ho ahau.

III. Ox ahau.

I. Hun ahau.

XII. Lahca ahau.

X. Lahun ahau.

VIII. Uaxac ahau: uchci puchtun ychpaa
Mayapan tumen u pach paa, u pach
tulum, tumen multepal ych cah Mayapan lal lae.

6.   VI. Uac ahau.

IIII. Can ahau: uchci mayacimlal; uchci
ocnakuchil ych paa.

II. Cabil ahau: uchci kakil nohkakile.

7. XIII. Oxlahun ahau; cimci Ahpula uacppel
haab; u binel u xocol haab ti lakin
cuchie; 'caanil kan cumlahci pop ti
lakin he tunte na cici pahool katun
haab; hun hix cip catac oxppeli Bolon ymix hi; u kinil lay cimci Ahpula lae napotxiu tu habil *D°.* 158
años.

8.   XI. Buluc ahau: hulciob kul uinicob ti lakin; u yah talzah; ulob u yaxchun
uay lae luumil coon maya uinice tu
habil *D°.* 1523 años.

IX. Bolon ahau: hoppci *xpnoil*; uchci ca-

¹ Canil.

putzihil; laytal ychil u katunil hulci
obispo tora 'ua; xane hauci ²huytabe
tu habil *D°*. 1546 años.

VII. Uuc ahau: cimci *obispo de Landa*.

V. Hoo ahau.

III. Ox ahau.

¹ uay.   ² chuytabe.

TRANSLATION.

This is the Record of the count of the katuns from when took place the discovery of Chichen Itza; this is written for the town in order that it may be known by whoever wishes to know as to the counting of the katuns.

1.   VI. In the sixth ahau took place the discovery of Chichen Itza.

IIII. This is the fourth ahau.

II. The second ahau.

XIII. The thirteenth ahau ; Pop was set in order.

XI. The eleventh ahau.

IX. The ninth ahau.

VII. The seventh ahau.

V. The fifth ahau.

III. The third ahau.

I. The first ahau.

XII. The twelfth ahau.

X. The tenth ahau ; Chichen Itza was

abandoned ; at this time it took place that thirteen divisions of warriors went to Chakanputun for houses.

---

2.   VI. The sixth ahau.

   IIII. The fourth ahau ; the land was taken in possession by those of Chakanputun.

    II. The second ahau.

 XIII. The thirteenth ahau.

  XI. The eleventh ahau.

  IX. The ninth ahau.

 VII. The seventh ahau.

   V. The fifth ahau.

  III. The third ahau.

   I. The first ahau.

 XII. The twelfth ahau.

  X. The tenth ahau.

VIII. The eighth ahau: Chakanputun was deserted by the men of Itza when they came in search of their houses for the second time ; thirteen divisions of warriors dwelt in the houses at Chakanputun ; in this katun those of Itza were under the trees, under the boughs, under the branches, to their misery.

3. VI. The sixth ahau.

IV. The fourth ahau.

II. The second ahau.

XIII. The thirteenth ahau.

XI. The eleventh ahau.

IX. The ninth ahau.

VII. The seventh ahau.

V. The fifth ahau.

III. The third ahau.

I. The first ahau.

XII. The twelfth ahau.

X. The tenth ahau.

VIII. The eighth ahau: the men of Itza were driven out of their houses a second time because of the plot of Hunac Ceel, because of the festivities with those of Itzmal; thirteen divisions of warriors dwelt there when they were driven out by Hunnac Ceel in order that those of Itza might know what was to be given.

4. VI. The sixth ahau.

IIII. The fourth ahau; the territory of the fortress of Mayapan was seized by

the men of Itza as also the houses
by those of Itzamal because of the
plotting - - - - of Hunnac Ceel.

5.   II. The second ahau.
    XIII. The thirteenth ahau.
     XI. The eleventh ahau.
     IX. The ninth ahau.
    VII. The seventh ahau.
      V. The fifth ahau.
    III. The third ahau.
      I. The first ahau.
    XII. The twelfth ahau.
      X. The tenth ahau.
   VIII. The eighth ahau: there was fighting
        in the fortress of Mayapan because
        of the seizure of the fortress and
        the fortified town by the joint gov-
        ernment in the city of Mayapan.

6.   VI. The sixth ahau.
      IV. The fourth ahau : the pestilence took
          place, the general death took place
          in the fortress.
      II. The second ahau ; the smallpox broke
          out.

7. XIII. The thirteenth ahau ; Ahpula died
          the sixth year ; the count of the years

was toward the east: (the month)
Pop began on 4 Kan to the east *
*   *   *   *   9 Imix was
the day on which Ahpula NapotXiu
died in the year of the Lord 158.

8.   XI. The eleventh ahau : the mighty men
came from the East, they brought the
sickness; they arrived for the first
time in this country we Maya men
say in the year 1513.

IX. The ninth ahau: Christianity began;
baptism took place; also in this katun arrived bishop Toral here; also
the hanging ceased in the year
1546.

VII. The seventh ahau ; bishop Landa died.

V. The fifth ahau.

III. The third ahau.

NOTES.

The writer states, in a brief introduction, the nature and purpose of his composition.

U kahlay, the record, or the memoir, from *kahal*, to remember. The concrete meaning of the root is " to know by sight, to recognize." *ɔiban*, past participle, passive voice, of *ɔib* to write : the original signification of the word is " to paint." *Yoheltabal*, passive form of *ohel*, to know, which is always conjugated with the pronominal prefixes, *u, a, y*. *Yolah*, syncopated form of *u uolah*, he wills, wishes, *uol = volo*, *uolah = voluntas*.

It will be noticed that this chronicle is not called an "arrangement" of the katuns, *tzolan katun*, but a count or reckoning of them, *xocan* or *xocol*, from *xoc*, to count.

1. The count begins with the discovery of Chichen Itza, mentions that Pop was " counted in order " at the beginning of the next following Ahau Katun, and having stated the desertion of Chichen Itza and the migration to Chakanputun, the chronicler draws a line, as if to separate broadly these occurrences from those which followed.

5. The distinction between *paa* and *tulum* appears to be that *tulum* is an enclosure surrounded by a defensive wall, and this wall itself; while *paa* is a castle, or, in Maya land, a mound or pyramid with buildings on it erected for purposes of defence.

6. *Kakil nohkakil,* the fire, the great fire, but here in the sense of a contagious febrile disease, probably the smallpox.

7. The text in this section is corrupt, and I leave a line untranslated. The writer informs us, what was omitted in the previous chronicles, that the Ahpula whose death is so carefully mentioned by all, was a member of the Xiu family which reigned over the province of Mani. They were almost the first of the powerful Maya nobles to make friends with the Spaniards. The date 158 is apparently intended for 1538, or perhaps 1508, which is more consistent with the following section, but less so with the previous chronicles.

Kul uinicob, as remarked on page 133, means "the mighty men," not the "holy men," as generally translated. The term was applied to the Spaniards. The *Dicc. de Motul* MS. says:—" KULVINIC: muy hombre, hombre de respeto y de hecho, y llaman así los Indios á los Españoles." *U yah talzah,* they bring the sickness, probably the smallpox. *Coon* or *con,* 1st pers. pl. pres. indic. of the irregular verb *cen* (*cihi, ciac*), to say, to tell.

IV. THE MAYA KATUNS.

From the Book of Chilan Balam of Chumayel,

The following chronicle is stated by its writer to be distinctively called the "Maya Katuns," and to be written for (or by) the Itzas. We have, therefore, no longer to do with the reckoning of the subjects of the Xiu family who ruled at Mani, but with one which emanates from the priests of the Cocomes, who were hereditary masters of Chichen Itza. It is evidently of different origin, although many of the same facts are referred to in it.

TEXT.

U kahlay katunob utial ahYtzaob maya-
katun u kaba lae.

---

1. Lahca ahau.
   Lahun ahau.
   Uaxac ahau.
   Uac ahau ; paxciob ahoni.
   Can ahau.
   Cabil ahau.
   Oxlahun ahau.
   Buluc ahau.
   Bolon ahau.
   Uuc ahau.
   Hoo ahau ; paxci u cah yahau ahYtzmal kin-
   ich kakmo *y* pop hol chan tumenel hun nac
   ceel.
   Ox ahau.
2. Hun ahau : paxci yala ahYtza tu chicheen,
   tu yoxpiztun ychil hun ahau paxci u chich-
   een.
   Lahca ahau.
   Lahun ahau.

3. Uaxac ahau: u katunil heɔci cah yala ahYtza likul yan che yalan haban tan xuluc mul u kaba ti likulob ca u heɔahob luum Zaclactun Mayapan u kaba tu uucpiztun uaxac ahau u katunil; laix u katunil cimci Chakanputun tumen kak u pa cal yetel tec uilue.

4. Uac ahau.

Can ahau.

Cabil ahau.

Oxlahun ahau.

Buluc ahau.

Bolon ahau.

Uuc ahau.

Hoo ahau: ulci ɔul ti chibil uinic, yxma pic ɔul u kaba; ma paxci peten tumenelobi.

Ox ahau.

5. Hun ahau: paxci peten tan cah mayapan u kaba tu hunpiztun ychil hun ahau u katunile; lukci halach uinic tutul *y* u Batabilob cabe *y* cantzuc culcahobe; lay u katunil paxi uincob tan cah ᴵcauec ²chahiob u Batabilob cabe.

6. Lahca ahau te cħabi Otzmal u tunile.

Lahun ahau, te cħabi Zizal u tunile.

ᴵ caua.   ² cahiob.

Uaxac ahau, te chabi Kancaba u tunile.

Uac ahau, te chabi hunnacthi u tunile.

7. Can ahau, te chabi atikuhe u tunilae; lay u
katunil uchci mayacimlal tu hopiztun ychil
can ahau u katunil lae.

Cabil ahau, te chabi chacalna u tunile.

Oxlahun ahau, te chabi euan u tunile.

8. Buluc ahau, u yaxchun kin coloxpeten chabi
u tunile; laix u katunil cimci Ahpula Napotxiu u kaba tu hunpiztun Buluc ahau.
Laix u katunil yax hulciob españolesob
uay tac lumil lae tu uucpiztun Buluc ahau
u katunil tiix hoppi xpnoil lae tu habil
quinientos diez y nueve años D° 1519 aˢ.

'9. Bolon ahau ma chabi u tunil lae; lay katun
yax ulci obispo Fray Franᶜᵒ ' to Ral, huli tu
uacpiztun ychil ahBolon ahau katun lae.

Uac ahau, ma chabi u tunil lae; lay u katunil cimci Obispo e landa lae, tii xuli uhel
Obispo xani.

Hoo ahau.

Ox ahau.

¹ Toral.

TRANSLATION.

The Record of the Katuns by the men of Itza called the Maya Katuns.

1. The twelfth ahau.

The tenth ahau.

The eighth ahau.

The sixth ahau; the well dressed ones were driven out.

The fourth ahau.

The second ahau.

The thirteenth ahau.

The eleventh ahau.

The ninth ahau.

The seventh ahau.

The fifth ahau; the town was destroyed by Kinich kakmo, ruler of Itzmal, and Pop Hol Chan on account of Hunnac Ceel.

The third ahau.

2. The first ahau; the remainder of the Itzas at

Chichen were driven out; on the third year in the first ahau Chichen was depopulated.

The twelfth ahau.

The tenth ahau.

3. The eighth ahau; in this katun was founded a city by the remainder of the Itzas coming out of the woods from under the branches, from the midst of Xuluc Mul as it is called; they came from there and established the land called Zaclactun Mayapan, in the seventh year of the eighth Ahau katun; in this katun perished Chakanputun by fire, which destroyed it quickly, and suddenly consumed it.

4. The sixth ahau.

The fourth ahau.

The second ahau.

The thirteenth ahau.

The eleventh ahau.

The ninth ahau.

The seventh ahau.

The fifth ahau; foreigners came seeking men to eat; "breechless foreigners" they were called: the country was not depopulated by them.

The third ahau.

5. The first ahau; the district in the middle of Mayapan (or Tancah Mayapan) was depopulated

in the first year of the first ahau katun; there went
forth the governor Tutul, with the chiefs of the
country and four divisions from the towns; in this
katun the men in the centre of the town (or of
Tancah) were driven out, and the chiefs of the
country lost their power.

6. The twelfth ahau: the stone of Otzmal was
taken.

The tenth ahau; the stone of Zizal was taken.

The eighth ahau; the stone of Kancaba was
taken.

The sixth ahau; the stone of Hunnacthi was
taken.

7. The fourth ahau; the stone of Ahtiku was taken; in this katun took place the pestilence, in the
fifth year in the fourth ahau katun.

The second ahau; the stone of Chacalna was
taken.

The thirteenth ahau; the stone of Euan was
taken.

8. The eleventh ahau: in the time of its beginning, the stone of Coloxpeten was taken; in this
katun died Ahpula Napotxiu, in the first year of
the eleventh ahau; it was also in this katun that
the Spaniards first arrived here in this land, in the
seventh year of the eleventh ahau katun; also Chris-

tianity began in the year fifteen hundred and nineteen, the year of our Lord 1519.

9. The ninth ahau ; no stone was taken at this time ; in this katun first came the bishop Brother Francisco Toral ; he arrived in the sixth year of the ninth ahau katun.

The seventh ahau ; no stone was taken : in this katun died Bishop Landa ; then also ended the bishop his successor.

The fifth ahau.

The third ahau.

NOTES.

1. The writer begins with the 12th ahau, although nothing is noted until the 6th. Here we have the brief entry *paxciob ahoni*. This might be translated "those of Oni were driven out or scattered." But no such locality is known or mentioned elsewhere. The *Diccionario de Motul, MS.* gives the meaning of *ahoni* as "pulido, galan, muy bien vestido," *ahoni a talel ex*, "you come very well dressed." I suppose, therefore, that it was a term applied to some early tribe who distinguished themselves in comparison with their ruder neighbors by elegance of costume. Later we shall find a similar term, "breechless foreigners," applied to another tribe whose condition of nudity suggested their appellation.

The name Kinich Kakmo is mentioned by Cogolludo as that of an idol worshiped at Itzamal. He says:—"They had another temple on another mound in the northern part of the city, and this, from the name of an idol which they worshiped here, they called *Kinich Kakmó*, which means the sun with a face. They say that the rays were of fire and descended at mid-day to consume the sacrifice, as the vacamaya flies through the air (which is a bird something like a parrot, though larger in size, and with finely colored feathers). They resorted to this idol in time of mortality, pestilence or much sickness, both men and women, and brought many offerings. They said that at mid-day a fire descended and consumed the sacrifice in the sight of all. After this the priests replied to their inquiries about the sickness, famine or pestilence, and thus they learned their fate; although it often turned out quite the contrary of what he predicted." (*Historia de Yucatan*, Lib. IV, cap. VIII.)

The title given by Cogolludo to the divinity appears to have also been adopted by the ruling chief, who may also have been the high priest. It is both imperfectly and incorrectly translated by the historian. Its components are *kin*, the sun, day; *ich*, the eye, the face; *kak*, fire; *moo*, the macaw, *Psittacus Macao*, deemed sacred throughout Mexico and Central America, on account of its beautiful plumage. The full translation of the name is "the Eye of Day, the Sacred Bird of Fire," a symbolic name of a solar deity.

The Chan family is mentioned by Sanchez Aguilar (*Informe contra Idolum Cultores*, etc.), as among the princely houses of Yucatan at the date of the Conquest.

Paxci u cah, "the town," that is, Chichen Itza. The writer composed his chronicle at that place, so he does not think it necessary to name it specifically. The distance in a straight line from Chichen Itza to Itzamal is 40 geographical miles.

2. *Yala*, the remainder, from *ala*, above, over. A portion of the Itzas remained in Chichen after the attack by Kinich Kakmo; these also now leave it.

3. The place *Xuluc mul* is unknown in the present geography of the peninsula. It means "the completed mounds," *mul* being, as I have before remarked, the name given to the artificial pyramids and tumuli of stone so common in the peninsula, probably so called from the joint labor of many in their construction.

The province of Zaclactun-Mayapan is also unknown,

although there is a hacienda Zaclactun within the boundaries of the modern district of Itzamal (Berendt, *Nombres geograficos en Lengua Maya*, MS.). The name apparently means "the place where white pottery is made."

4. *Ti chibil uinic* "for men to be eaten;" *chibil*, the passive of *chii*, to eat. The *Diccionario de Motul* gives *chibil bak*, flesh to be eaten. *Pic* was the breech cloth or waist cloth, fastened around the waist and falling to the knees, which was the common dress of the women. The Dictionary just quoted translates the word, "naguas de Indias que se sirven de saya ó faldellin ordinario, para cubrir desde la cintura abajo; y son las blancas sin color ni bordado." The phrase *ixma pic ɔul*, foreigners without a breech cloth, intimates that they were nude.

Who were these naked cannibals, who raided the provinces in order to obtain their unnatural food? Those daring navigators, those naked man-eaters, the Caribs, from whose name our word *cannibal* is derived, at once suggest themselves. Curiously enough, the Abbe Brasseur has argued for the probability of their invasions upon other (though I think insufficient) grounds (see his *Informe acerca de las Ruinas de Mayapan y de Uxmal*). This passage of the chronicle renders his theory probable.

5. *Peten tan cah Mayapan* could also be rendered, "the district Tancah Mayapan."

6. *Chabi Otzmal u tunile*, "the stone of Otzmal was taken." Otzmal was a locality under the rule of the Cocomes. (Cogolludo, *Historia*, Lib. III, cap. VI.) Other versions read Itzmal and Uxmal. The reference is to the *u heɔ katun*, the setting up of the Katun-stone as a memorial at the end of each period of twenty years. Incomplete descrip-

tions of this ceremony are given by Landa, *Relacion*, § IX, and Cogolludo, *Historia*, Lib. IV, cap. IV. I propose a more extended examination of this question in a future volume of this series, devoted to documents relating to the calendars and chronology of the Central American nations.

8. The death of Ahpula Napot Xiu is given with minuteness but not in accordance with previous chronicles. In 1519 Cortes touched at the Island of Cozumel, and that might have been assumed as the date of the commencement of Christianity.

V. THE CHIEF KATUNS.

From the Book of Chilan Balam of Chumayel.

———

The document which follows is brief, but of peculiar interest. It does not appear to aim at a connected history of events, but in the form of a chant to refer certain incidents to the katuns in which they occurred. It has more of a mythological character, and the repetitions remind one of the refrain of a song.

It is also found in the Book of Chilan Balam of Chumayel, and is inserted without explanation or introduction, copied, no doubt, from some ancient writing.

1. Can ahau u kaba katun; uchci u zihilob——
   [1] pauaha en cuh u yahauob.

2. [2] Oxhunte ti katun lic u tepalob, lay u kabaob
   tamuk u tepalob lae.

3. Can ahau u kaba katun; emciob [3] noh hemal,
   [4] ɔeemal, u kabaob lae.

4. Oxlahunte ti katun, lic u tepalob, lic u kabati-
   cob, ti i ualac u cutob. Oxlahun cuthi, u
   cutob lae.

5. Can ahau u katunil; uchci u caxanticob
   u chicħeen Ytzua; tii utzcinnahi mactzil
   tiob tumen u yumoobe. Cantzuc lukciob
   cantzucul cab u kabaob; likul ti likin kin
   colah peten bini huntzuci; [5] kul xaman naco
   cob [6] hok huntzucci; heix hoki huntzucci holtun çuyuua ti chikin; hoki huntzuccie canhek
   uitz, bolonte uitz u kaba u luumil lae.

6. Can ahau u katunil [7] uhci u payalob tu cant-
   zuccilob can tzuccul cab u kabaob, ca emiob tu
   chicħeen Ytzae ahYtza tun u kabaob. Ox-

---

[1] pachah u cah.   [2] oxlahunte.   [8] nohemel.
[4] ɔeɔemel.   [5] likul.   [6] hoki.   [7] uchci.

lahunte ti katun, lic u tepalob; ca oci u ke-
banthanobi tumen hunnac ceeli.   Ca paxci
u calob. Ca biniob tan yol che tan xuluc mul,
u kaba.   Can ahau u katunil; uchci yauat
pixanobi.   Oxlahunte ti katun lic u tepalobi
y u numyaobi.

7. Uaxac ahau u katunil; uchci yulelob yalaob
   ahYtza u kabaob.   Ca ulob tii ca ualac u tepalob Chakanputun.   Oxlahun ahau u ka-
   tunii u heɔob cah mayapan mayauinic u kabaob.   Uaxac ahau paxci u cahobi; ca uacc-
   habi ti peten tulacal. Uac katuni paxiob,
   ca haui u Maya kabaob.   Buluc ahau u kaba
   u katunil hauci u maya kabaob; Maya uinicob Christiano u kabaob tulacal u cuchcabal
   tzo ma Sanc Pedro y Rey ahtepale.

TRANSLATION.

1. The fourth ahau was the name of the katun; the births took place;—; the towns were taken possession of by the rulers.

2. It was the thirteenth katun in which they ruled; these were their names while they ruled.

3. The fourth ahau was the name of the katun; in it they arrived, the Great Arrival, the Less Arrival, as they are called.

4. It was the thirteenth katun in which they ruled, in which they took names, at that time, while they resided here; in the thirteenth the residence was continued, they resided here.

5. The fourth ahau katun; then took place the search for Chichen Itza; at that time they were marvelously improved by the fathers. They went forth in four divisions which were called the four territories. One division came forth from the east of Kin Colah Peten; one division came forth from the north of Nacocob; one division came forth from the gate of Zuyuua to the west; one division came forth from the mountains of Canhek, the Nine Mountains, as the land is called.

6. The fourth ahau katun; then took place the calling together of the four divisions, the four territories as they were called, and they arrived at Chichen Itza and were called the men of Itza. It was the thirteenth katun in which they ruled; then the plottings were introduced by Hunnac Ceel, and the territories were destroyed. Then they went into the midst of the forests, into the midst of Xuluc Mul, so called. The fourth ahau katun; then singing for their happiness took place. It was the thirteenth katun in which they governed and had heavy labor.

7. The eighth ahau katun; thus it took place that there arrived the remainder of the Itza men as they were called; then they arrived; and about that time they governed Chakanputun. In the thirteenth ahau katun those called the Maya men founded the city Mayapan. In the eighth ahau the towns were destroyed; then they were driven wholly out of the province. In the sixth katun they were destroyed, and it was ended with those called Mayas. It was the eleventh ahau katun in which it ended with those called Mayas. The Maya men were all called Christians and came under the control of Saint Peter and the King, the rulers.

1. *U zihilob,* the births, probably meaning the beginning of things. *Pauaha en cuh* has no meaning that I can make out ; I therefore suppose it an error for *pachah u cah,* and translate in accordance with this emendation. The phrase seems to refer to the first settlement of the country, or to the first time the scattered inhabitants were gathered together in towns by their chiefs.

2. "These were their names"; but no names are given. They seem to have been omitted by the copyist.

3. *Emciob noh hemal ɔeemal,* faulty orthography for *noh emel, ɔeemel,* the latter syncopated from *ɔeɔemel.* Literally, "since they descended; the Great Descent, the Little Descent."

The tradition here referred to is given at more length by Father Lizana, in his *Historia de Yucatan,* and is discussed also by Cogolludo (*Historia de Yucatan,* Lib. IV, cap. III). As the work of the former is wholly inaccessible, I quote from the reprint of a portion of it in Brasseur's edition of Diego de Landa's *Relacion* p. 354. "In former times they called the East *Cen-ial,* the Little Descent, and the West *Nohen-ial,* the Great Descent. The reason they give for this is that on the east of this land a few people descended, and on the west a great many ; and with that syllable they understand little or much, to the east and the west; and that few people came from one direction and many from the other." Father Liz-

ana goes on to express his opinion that the few who came
from the East were the Carthaginians, and the many from the
West were the Mexicans.

The very corrupt form in which he has given the words has
led Señor Eligio Ancona to suppose they belonged to the archaic and secret language of the priests (*Historia de Yucatan*,
Tomo I, p. 24), and Dr. Carl Schultz-Sellack to imagine that
they referred to East and West, right and left, as he adopted
the misreading *ɔiic*, left, for *ɔeɔ*, little (*Die Amerikanischen
Götter der Vier Weltgegenden*, in the *Archiv für Ethnologie*,
Band XI, 1879). But they are readily analyzed when we
have their correct orthography, as given above. The reference to them in this place shows that the author of the
chant was dealing with the most ancient legends of his race.

The Itzas who resided in the Peten district left the region
around Chichen Itza some time in the fifteenth century,
probably after the fall of Mayapan. They were ruled by an
hereditary chieftain, called by the Spaniards "the great king,
Canek." Under him the territory was divided into four
districts, each with its own chief, with whom the Canek con-
sulted about important undertakings.

Evidently in removing to Peten the Itzas were retracing
their steps on the line of their first entrance to the peninsula.
They even attempted to go further west, and guided, probably,
by ancient memories, a large number set out for Tabasco and
the banks of the Usumaciuta, where repose the ruins of
Palenque, possibly the home of their ancestors. But they
were attacked and driven back by the natives of Tabasco,·
with the loss of their leader, a brother-in-law of the great
Canek. These and other particulars about them are repeated

by Villagutierre Sotomayor, *Historia de la Conquista de la Provincia de el Itza*, folio, Madrid, 1701.

4. The elliptical form of expression here renders the translation difficult. The verb *cutal* (old form *cultal*), pret. *culhi* or *cuthi*, fut. *culac*, means to sit down, to remain in a place, to be at home there, to reside, etc. Perhaps the translation both here and in § 2 should be, "for thirteen katuns they ruled, etc."

5. The word *yum*, plural *yumob*, means father and also chief, leader, ruler, etc. In modern Maya it is the translation of Sir, Mister, Señor.

The proper names of the localities whence the four divisions are said to have come, have a mythological cast. I cannot find any of them in the present geography of Yucatan. Kin Colah Peten is mentioned in a "katun wheel" in this same Book of Chilan Balam of Chumayel, as the name of one of the towns which furnished a katun stone. Zuiva I have already referred to as appearing in the Quetzalcoatl myth (see page 110).

The mountains of Canhek and the Nine Mountains take us to the Itzas around Lake Peten, in the extreme south of the peninsula, this last mentioned division being, in fact, that from the south.

6. *U payalob*, plural passive of *pay*, to call, to summon.

Tan yol che, ol or *yol* is the heart or centre of the leaf or plant; *tan xuluc mul*, see page 174. *Yauat pixanobi*, they were happy in singing, or, they gained favor by singing. The expression is obscure. The verb *auat* is applied to the singing of birds, the crowing of cocks, and generally to the natural sound made by any animal, and, in composition, to the sound of musical instruments, as, *auatzah*, to play on the flute, to blow a trumpet.

7. *Uacchahi* from *uacchahal*, appears to be a strongly figurative expression. It is explained in Pio Perez' Dictionary, "salirse con esfuerzo de su cubierta ó encaje, saltarse de ella *como tripa por el ano.*"

Hauic, from *haual*, to end, finish, cease to exist. Thus the chronicler closes his recital, repeating the to him no doubt bitter fact that the Maya nation and the Maya name had passed away.

THE CHRONICLE

OF

Chac Xulub Chen.

BY

NAKUK PECH.

1562.

CHRONICLE OF CHICXULUB.

Among the ancient documents collected by Pio Perez was a series relating to the town of Chicxulub, about six leagues north of Merida. They are entitled *Documentos de Tierras de Chicxulub, 1542.* They consist of a history of the town and of the conquest of the country, written by Nakuk Pech, about 1562; a survey of the town lands by several members of the Pech family, testified to Feb. 7, 1542; a partial list of the Spanish conquerors; a portion of an account by another member of the Pech family, and a further statement by Nakuk Pech.

The longest and the most interesting of these is the history of the Conquest, or, as the writer calls it, "the history and the chronicle of Chacxulubchen"—*u belil u kahlail Chac Xulub Chen*—this being one of the native forms of the name of the town. It is headed "Conquest and Map," but the map has disappeared. Usually such "maps" accompanying the title papers of towns in Yucatan have as a central figure the outlines of a church with the name of the town; around this is drawn the figure of the town lands, with the names of the wells, trees, stones and other landmarks mentioned in the titles.

The writer, Nakuk Pech, baptized Pablo Pech, must have been between sixty and seventy years of age when he drew up his statement, inasmuch as he mentions occurrences as late as 1562, and also speaks of himself as an adult in 1519. He belonged to a noble family, the Pechs of Cumkal, who are mentioned by Sanchez Aguilar as hereditary *batabs*, or independent chiefs. They appear to have given their names to the province on the west coast called Kin Pech, or Campech, known to the English as Campeachy, and to that of Ceh Pech, in which the city of Ho, afterwards called Merida, was situated. The Abbe Brasséur, on very slight grounds, surmised that they were not originally of Maya stock, but probably descendants of the Caribs.[1]

He states that he was the son of Ak Kom Pech, in baptism Martin Pech, and the grandson of Ah Tunal Pech, while the head of the house of Pech seems to have been Ah Naum Pech, baptized Don Francisco de Montejo Pech.

[1] See his *Informe acerca de las Ruinas de Mayapan y de Uxmal.*

Pech always uses as the name of his town *Chac Xulub Chen,* which means "the well of the great horns," probably because some huge antlers were found there, or were set up to mark the spot. The modern name *Chic Xulub* was probably applied to it as a parody, or a play on words. It means to cuckold one, to put horns on him.[1]

A literal translation of the document was made by Don Manuel Encarnacion Avila, of Merida, about 1860, and this has been of service to me in completing the present rendering. But Señor Avila, though familiar with the Maya of to-day, was evidently not at all acquainted with the ancient terms with reference to the calendar, and the usages of the natives before the Conquest. He therefore made serious errors wherever such occurred.

Moreover, as it was his purpose to give an extremely literal translation, he often sacrificed to this both clearness and correctness, and in various passages his sentences are unintelligible.

The Abbé Brasseur (de Bourbourg) commenced to copy the original when in Merida, but completed only the first two paragraphs. He applied for a

[1] "CHIJCXULUB: poner los cuernos; hacer cabron á uno; *u chiicah bin u xulub u lak;* diz que pusó los cuernos á su compañero ô proximo; que se aprobechó de su muger ô manceba," *Diccionario de Motul, MS.*

copy of the remainder; but by an error he received instead of this an unfinished transcript of another paper by the Pech family. These fragments he inserted, with a translation of his own, in the second volume of the Reports of the *Mission Scientifique au Mexique et à l'Amérique Centrale*, pp. 110-120 (4 to, Paris, Imprimerie Impériale: 1870). As his lexicographic resources were, by his own statement, quite deficient (*id.*, note to p. 116), he is scarcely to be criticised if, as is the case, much of his translation but faintly presents the meaning of the original.

It will be seen that I have sacrificed every attempt at elegance in the English translation to an endeavor to preserve faithfully the style of the original, even to its needless repetitions and awkward sentences.

Concixta yetel Mapa.

---

1. U hotzuc ca culhi ah buluc ahau lai katun ca uli
Españolesob ca cahiob te ti noh cah te ti Ho ; lae
te ix ah bolon ahaue ti tun cahi cristianoili ; lae
he hab yax ulci ca yum Españolesob uay ti lum
lae tu habil 1511 años.

---

2. Ten cen yn Nakuk Pech yax hidalgos concixtadoren, uay ti lum lae tu cacabil Maxtunil cin
ɔabal ti yax cah tu cacabil chacxulub Chen. Bai
bic ɔaa nen in canante tumen in yumob Ah Naum
Pech lic utzcinic utz olal u belil u kahlail uay ti
cacab Chac Xulub Chen in yax mekthantah lai
cah lae capel cacab Chichinica y uay Chaac Xulub
Chen.

3. Cen Nakuk Pech in kaba cuchi ti ma ococ
haa tin pol cuchi u mehenen Tahkom Pech Dᵒⁿ
Martin Pech ti cah Xulkum Cheel; bai bic ɔaanoon
canan hol cacabob tumen in yum Ah Naum Pech
likul tu cah Mutul ca tah culcintaben in canante
cacab Chac Xulub Chen lae ti manan to u manac

u talel ca yum Españolesob uay tac lumi Yucatan
lae ten tun halach uinic uai ti cah uai ti luum Cħac
Xulub Cħen lae ca tun uli ca yum Sr.   Adelantado uai ti peten lae ichil yabil 1519 años cuchi lae
ten ix yax batab; ca uli Españolesob tu lumil uai
Maxtunil lae toonix kame tu yabal ɔaolalobe toonix yax ɔaic patan yetel ɔicil tiob y ca ɔaic hanalob tiob capitanob Españolesob; hek Adelantado u kabae
lai uli uai Maxtunil tu tancabal Nachi May; ti yanob ca binon cilob uchebal ca ɔaic cicioltiob; may-
to ococob ti cah cuchi chenbel zutucahob paibe
uai ti lume oxppel u ɔanlob uai tu cacabil Maxtunile uai tun likulob cu binelob tu holpai ɔunul tu
hol u payil ɔilam tancoch yoxpel hab cahanobi.

4. Tiob yan cuchi ca bini u kubulte in yumob
tiob; lai Adelantado u kaba lai zutui uai ti lum;
lae Ixkakuk u kaba u ɔa in yum tiob lai u kaba lai
xcħuplal u ɔah tiob menyahticob y tzenticob tiob
tan yan cuchi ca tal katuntabilob tumen Cupulob
ca tun lukobi ca biniob ti cahtalob ti Ecab kantanenkin u kaba u lumil cahlahciob; tix yanob cuchi ca
katuntabiob tumen Ah Ecabob ca lukobie ca cuchob Cauaca ti tun oꞇcobi te maniob ti cah [1] ɔekom
ti u kaba cuhe manciob ca cuchiob ti cah Tixcuum-
cuUuc u kaba cah kuchciob ti liculob ca kuchoob

---

[1] Tekom.

Tinuum u kaba cah kuchciob caix u tzaclahob u
Chichen Ytza u kaba ti tun u katahob u Rey cah
u lahanobi ca alab tiobi: " Yan ahau, yume," ci
yalalob, "ye yan Ahau Cocom Aun Pech Ahau
Pech, Namox Cheel Ahau Cheel ɔiɔan tun ; Katun
ɔul, te xebnae," ci yalalob tumen ᶠ naob Bon Cupul ; u lukulob tu Chicheen Ytza lae catun cuchiob
yicnal Ahau Ixcuat Cocom te Akee : " Yume, ma-
tab a binelex te lae ; bin zatacex," cibin yalablob
tumen Ahau Ixcuat Cocom ca ualkahiob tutulpa-
chob, ca binob ca cuchob Cauaca tu caaten, caix
kuchob tu holpayal Catzim u kaba tix nakob ti
kankabe, ca biniob ti cahtalob tuyulpachob tet ɔelebnae u kabae lai yax cahicob ca ulob uai ti luum
lae.

5. Lai ye tan Chanpatune uacppel hab cahanobi
caix u hokzahubaob te Campeche ; lai Adelantado
u kaba yax ɔule lai mani uai ti lum ; lae tiob tun
yan Campech cuchi ca u katahob patan caix u yabi
u thanob tumen batabob tu cahalcahobe tulacal bini patan ; tiob te maaniob ti kaknabe yahpulul patanob ; lae ca tun binen *y* in lakob Ah MaCamPech
y u yit ɔin Ixkil Ytzam Pech in yahaulil cah Cum-
kale *y* in yum yan ti cah Xulcum Cheele ; lai in
lakob cat binen tu pach patan, laix ca yilahob, laix

ᶠ nacon Cupul.

ca alak Nachi May, yoklal yohel maa yohel ma u
thanob yoklal u yax ulob ichil yotoch, ca uliob lae
laitah oklal u thanahob u lakintob, ca binob tu pach
patan yoklal yettail tahiob Españolesob ti tun ku-
biob tumenel capitanobe ; tiix c ʼmatanok zayo *y*
capote *y* zapato *y* u *y* ppoc cicialtabion tumen te
capitanob ; caix lukon ca ɔoci ca ɔaic zililob Españolesob yan tacix ca buc ca ulon lay zayo *y* capote,
lay Ixkil Ytzam Pech yan Conkale laix ca lakah
Macan Pech yan Yaxkukule *y* in yum Ahkom
Pech u noxibal ca binon.

6. Cen ix Nakuk Pech lae in ḳaba ten yax batab yax kubob patan ca binon Campech ca kubob
patan, caix uloon tutul pache tamuk u talel Españolesob tu bel Campech talel u cahob ti cahtal Ich
can zi hoo ti nohcah ti Hoe ; tuchi ix ca yubah u
talelob Españolesob tu bel Campech, ca binon ca
ɔab ziltiob tolo ten caix binon tu caaten cat kube
patan.   Cen ix Nakuk Pech uai tu cabil Cħac
Xulub Cħen *y* Ah Macan Pech yan tu cabil Yax
Kukul *y* Ixkil Ytzam Pech u noh batabil Conkale *y*
ten cen Ixnakuk Pech batab uai ti cah Cħac Xulub Cħen teix oci ca ziltiob tucaaten te ɔibkale[1] ix
u chucan u nahubaob tucaaten ca ḳube ziltiob u
lum *y* cab *y* u cħahucil hanalob u kamciob te ɔibil-

<hr/>

[1] matanon.   [1] Tipikal.

kale ti tamuk u talel yocolob ti cahtal ti Hoo lay
Dⁿ Fran^{co} de Montejo, yax capitan General yax
ùli uai tu peten ti Hoo lae *y* Dⁿ Fran^{co} de Bracamonte y Fran^{co} Tamayo *y* Juan de Pacheco *y* Perarberes lai capitanesob uliob ichil habil 1541 años.

7. Lai hab ca uliob ti Hoo ti cahtalob lay capitanob mektanmail Españolesob, ca uliob ti Ho
lae tenili batab cen Ix Nakuk Pech, ca uli Españolesob te ti Hooe tenix kubi patan ti concixtadoresob ti Hoo, tenix batab uai ti cacab Chac Xulub
Chen lae tamuk u escribanoil Roderigo Alvares
ichil yabil 1542 años.

8. U tan u toxol cahob ti concixtadoresob tumen
capitanob adelantado lay yax Españolesob *y* escribano Roderigo Alvares lai ɔibtic u xocaan patanob
ti yulel hun huntzuc ti cahob, baix tamuk u kubic
patan in lakob tulacal lai in chibalob lae ti tamuk
ban patane yoklal toxbil patan tiob Españolesob
tumen capitanob adelantado *y* escribano Rodrigo
Alvarez ichil hun hunteel hab uli Españolesob ti
Hoo; tulacal ca ix chaben cen Ix Nakuk Pech ca
ɔaben ti Don Julian Doncel encomendero lai u
yax yumil cah uay Chaac Xulub Chen lae lai yax
encomendero, caix machi in kab *y* tu tan capitan
Don Fran^{co} de Montejo adelantado ten tun ɔabi ti
batabil ti Dⁿ Julian Donsel tu kab, ca hoppi in tan
lic u patan u yumil kul uinicilob.

9. Cen Ix Nakuk Pech lae ten tan lic in batabil cuchi ca uli Albares yax alcalde mayor uai tu
petenil Yucatan ti Hoo lae, caix uli Alvara de
Carvayor alcalde Mayor, li xan caix uli Oidor D^n
Tomas Lopez tenili batab cuchie heix in kabatah
cen ix Nakuk Pech ca oci ha tin pole y ca tin ka-
ma bautismo D^n Pablo Pech lay in kaba ca hau [1] in
kabatic Nakuk Pechil; hidalgoson yax batabon
tumen capitanob cat yax chuca uai ti peten lae ton
ix yax kubob patan ti ɔulob cat ɔab u chucil toon
tumen Dios y Rey ahtepal; lae ton u chibalon hidalgos tu yalomal in mehenob tulacal tu tan kinil
cu binel tu nak u hayalcab; lae ton batabon yahau-
biI uai ti luum ti ma yanac Santa Yglesiaob ti cacabob, tan to u ximbal tabal lumob tumen Españolesob uatub ci tan u moltalob utial u kulteob ti yoklal piz uinicob cuchi ti ma christianacobi tulacal
in mektan cahil uinicob tumen in kamci in Cristianoil, cen Nakuk Pech cuchi laili batab en cuchi ca in
kamah Santo Oleos y Santo ocolal, utial in cam-
zic in mektan cahilob tulacal tenix yax mache vara
utial justiciail, tumen t binen in nant u than Dios y
ca noh Ahau Rey Ahtepal; laitun ca yum ti Oidor
D^n Tomas Lopes ca uchi lae yax ɔai u xicin patan
ti batabob ti cahal cahob; lai temes ti ca yatan ɔooc-

[1] hauah.

tun yahaubil Oidor Dⁿ Tomas Lopes ca tun tin ku-
bah in bara ti in mehen Dⁿ Pedro Pech ichil habil
152 aˢ.

10. Lai cu xocol yabil cuchi lae ca in kamah u bara in yum Nakuk Pech Dⁿ Pablo Pech Ursula Pech
ixan uai ti cacab Chac Xulub Chen, lae utial in
meyactic Dios *y* ca noh ahau Rey ahtepal utial in
mektantic lai cah lae uai ti cacab Chac Xulub Chen
lae.

11. La tun ulicob tu cahalob yetel u yahkulelob *y*
u holpopob bay tu cahal Yaxkukul, bay tu cahal
Xulkum Cheel, bai tu cahal Maxtunil yaxchibal
Macan Pech yaxchibal Tahkom Pech Xulkum
Cheel, yet ulcob ix yahkinob yaxchibal Macan Pech
yaxchibal Tahkom Pech Xulkum Cheel, yet ulcobix
u cuchulob tu pachob, ca uliob uai ti cahtale yet
ulcobix yahkinob u holpopob *y* yahkulelob tu
pachob u halach uinicob, ca uliob tu cacabil Yaxkukul baix toon xan cat uloon uai tu cacabil Chac
Xulub Chen lae, ca cahiob uai lae lai culcinaben Tah
Nakuk Pech, tumen in yum Tah Koon Pech u
mehen Tah Tunal Pech yaxchibal Maxtunile
mektantic cah.

12. Lae cat uli ɔulob uai tu lumil cacabob lae
manan Maya uinicob ti kuchi yolob u kube patan
ti yax ɔulob cuchi, lae lai u yax cantahob ɔulob

Españolesob ɔocan ili tun u ɔabal cah canante. Cen tah Nakuk Pech in yax kamici cah uai ti cacab Cħac Xulub Cħen, ca uliob u chun u thanob tu pachob *y* yahkulel *y* u holpopob *y* yahkinob lae, lai u kaba Ah Kul Matu *y* Kulche *y* ulcob ix yax kinob Ahkin Cocom Ahkin Tacu *y* ulcob ix u holpop Nachan Cen *y* holpop Xuluc, lai u kaba, holpop lai mektanmailob ca ulob uai tii u lum Maxtunil *y* Ah Kul Chuc *y* u holpop tu pachob ; lai u heɔahob u cacabil uai Cħac Xulub Cħen caix uliob u holcanob u nacomob, nacom Kan, nacom Xuluc, nacom Pot, nacom May, nacom Ek, lai u kaba nacomob, layobi u kab nacomob yah mektanul batab tah Nakuk Pech ca ulen uai ti cah Cħac Xulub Cħen ; lai chiccunic yol lai in cu uchulob cat ulen uai ti cahtah uai ti luum uai tu cacabil Cħac Xulub Cħen.

13. Cen tah Nakuk Pech lae ca ulen tumen u halach uinic tenob ca chichi cah uai ti Cħac Xulub Cħen ; lae tumen u nucteelob cuchi lae manan u manak u talel Españolesob uai ti luum, lae minan u yana cah chicunic cah uai Cħac Xulub Cħen ; lai yobi t ubahilob lae ti xocan ili, yulel Españolesob ti noh cah ti Ho, *y* u kamal cristianoil tumen uinicob uai Tah Ceh Peche ɔocan ili ix in molic cah uai tulacahal Cħac Xulub Cħen, cen Dⁿ Pablo Pech

y in yum Dⁿ Martin Pech, conquixtador, Xulkum Cheel.

14. Lae ti tum lae ti hoppi u licil u katun Espa-ñolesob ich mul cochleah[1] ca binon, *y* in yum Ah Macan Pech yaxchibal Yaxkukul, y Yxkil Yɔam Pech yaxchibal Cumkal, *y* ti binen tu pach katun; ca oci u patan kooch uahobe lai tun mektanmai u yumil kul uiniclob cah, ca ti binon ti katun yah, yukul kah *y* tuce tumenel u kuxilob ti kul uinicob; ichil uacpe u yanonie *y* in lakob tu pach kul uini-cob ti numia; mektanan tun in yum tumen u chun-thanob, lay yobi hach ilaob yuchul tulacal tu banalob tin cantah ichil in informacion tulacal lae uchebal yoheltabal tumen in chibalob in mehenob tin pach ti uchen cimic uai okolcab[2] lae yoklal in titulo in probanza ɔaan ten tumen ca yumil ti Dios *y* ca noh Ahau Rey ahtepal; manan in patan maix uchac in botic patan maix in mehenob maix in u ixmehenob bin u bote patan yoklal tu lukzah ten ca yumil ti Dios ichil u zahacil in puczical; ti mato in uilal u uich Españolesob cuchi tu ɔahten ich ich olal utial in kubic inba tu kab Españolesob *y* in cahalob tulacal utial u cahal cahob tumenel capi-tanob Adelantado yax concixtadoresob; uliob uai ti

---

[1] cochlahal.   [2] yokolcab.

u lumil Yucatane; he hab yax ulci ɔulob tu lumil
uai ti Cupule lae 1511 años.

15. Cuchi mahun ilabac ɔulob Españolesob ca
chuci Jeronimo de Aguilar tumenob a Cusamilob;
lai lae u chun yohelabal peten tulacal lae yoklal
ɔoci u xinbaltabal uchi lumob tulacal, lai tah oklal
ma talan uchi lumob peten tulacal lai tun cin
ɔolic[1] tu tan Ahau ca tu cuchi tu tan Ahau Ah
Macan Pech Dⁿ Pedro Pech y u cuchteelob yax
chibaloḅ u nacomob tu pachob tulacal binob tu pach
yoklal utzilob Ahau ylal u uichob u maseual uinicob; caix tu te ta lahun cakal u nucil uinicob u
bines tu pach ti Ahau Rey ahtepal u tzicob ti
messa nachi ti España, heix mac xenahi[2] tu tzicile
tu tan Rey ahtepale; lai tun tu yala Ahau ca u
bote patanob tulacal, yal u mehenob tulacal, heix
ton Ah Pechob yaxchibal uai ti lum y yaxchibal
tal ti Cupul, ca bin tu yalaḥ yabil peten y yabil
maya uinicob u bal lum, caix bin tu tzolah u xocan
tu tanil ca noh Ahau ca uɔac[3] u talel heɔbil u chi
lum u Chinante Ahau; bay tun chacanhic ca lumil
lae lai Aguilar, lae te hantabi tumen ah Naum Ah
Pot Cusamile tu yabil 1517 años; lai yabil hauic
cha katun, lae lai hauic u uacuntabal u tunil balcah,
yoklal hunhunkal tun u talel uaatal u tunil balcah

---

[1] tzolic.   [2] xanhi.   [3] utznac.

cuchi ti man uluc ɔul Españolesobe Cusamil cuchi uaital petenil; tumen ulic Españolesob ca t haui u betabal.

16. 1519 años lai yabil yax ulcob Españolesob uai Cusamil tu yox mal, Fernando de Cortes *y* Espoblaco Lara. A 28 de Febrero cuchi ca uliob Cusamilob u yax mal ahohelilob hahal u cibel than. Lai yabil cuchcob tu Chicħen tah mak opile ti tun yax oheltabi u Chicħeen Ytza tumen noh Españolesob D^n Fran^co de Montejo Adelantado, u halach uinicob ca ɔanob tu Chicħen Ytza.

17. 1521 años tu yoxlahunpiz u kinil agosto chucic u lumil Mexico tumen Españolesob; uchci u yox katun tabalob [1] Españolesob tumen cah tulacal uai tu cahal Cupule; cauthi katahob Ah Ceh Pech tu cimil Zalibna *y* etahau Lenpot Tixkocħoh tu provinciail Ticanto *y* yicnal ah Kinichkakmo Ytzmal u nup u than holtun Ake; lai yabil lae uchic u kuchul Españolesob tu Chicħeen Ytza tu caten u heɔob u Chicħen Ytza, ti ca uli Capitan D^n Fran^co de Montejo yahtohil yahtochil Naocom Cupul kuchal u cah. Hunkal hab yax kuchcob tu Chicħen Ytza ti u kabahob ah makopilobe ah ɔuɔopob.

18. 1542 años lai hab ca u heɔahob lum Espan-

[1] tubalob.

olesob ti Hich can Ziho chuncan u nup u than Kinich Kakmo ahkin *y* Ahtutul Xiu yahaulil cabecera
Mani u pol u meta u heɔahob yaxcħibalob, lai yax
hoppic yocol patan tiob lae tu yoxten tun yulelob
ta lumil, ca tun hunkul culhob, lae heklai culicob;
helelae u hunten, ulcobe tu Chicħen Ytzae ti u yax
makahob oop, matech u makal lai oop, ca u maka-
hop Espanolesob u kabatcob ahmakoopilob; u caten ulcobi tu Chicħene ca ¹u tocahob naobon Cupul; tu yoxten yulelobe ca tun hunkul culhiob lae
lai yabil lae 1542 años lai tun hunkul culhiob uai ti
lum Ychcanzi hoo—yanilob, helelae oxlahun Kan
ahcuchhab ti Maya xoclae.

19. 1543 años lai yabil binci Españolesob tet
xaman Cheile u xachete Mayab uinicob u maseu-
altobe yoklal manan maseual uinic u palilob ti Ho;
¹ai talob ti xache uinicob u maseualtob tu chi tun,
ca kuchob ti Popce ti uch ban patan tiobi likulob ti
Ho, cat kuchob ti Popce tu chi, ca ulob ca biniob
Tikom, man ti kin yanhicobe te Tixkome ti hum-
kal u kinil yanob ca lukabi lai Españolesob.

20. Lae 1544 años lai hab ca ɔan ɔul Cauaca
Asiesa u capitanil, ca ɔanoob te Cauacae ti u chi
pach yumili ² ti oki patan tiobi cab ulum ixim ɔab-
tiob tiob yan Cauacae, catun ca tu kalahob ti mas-

¹ yotochob nacon.　　　　　² tiobi.

cab ahkul Caamal tal Sisal ca tu kata u xocal cah
tulacal, hun hab tialan ti mazcab tumenob, lai paye
u bel Españolesob ca taliob ti cahtal Sachi, heclai
Ahkul Kamal lae lai oci ti batabil Saci Sisale Dⁿ
Juan Caamal de la Cruz u kabatah yoklal hach
hahal u than, lai yax utzcit Cruz Cauacae, u yabi
u than tumen ɔulob, lae lai tumen lai ti oci ti batabil Sisal, ontkin ac u batabil cat cimil; lai ti pay u
bel Españolesob ca binob ti katun yah Tixkochnah;
xane he ɔulob lae hunppel hab ɔananob Cauaca,
lukob cat talob Saci hunkul hi u kal uinicob ti
mazcab yilab batab Caamal.

21. Lae 1545 años ɔaniɔulob Saci laix yabil hopp ·
ti cristianoil tumen padresob orden de San Franᶜᵒ,
te tu holhaa Champotone hali yax ulcob padresob
u machmaob cahlohil ti Jehucristo tu kabob lai lic
yezic ti maseual uinicob, cat yax ulob tu tu holhaa
Chanpoton, lae te chikin uai tu cuchcabal u than
uai Ichcansihoo, ti Hoo tu cahal Ichcansihoo lai u
kaba; lai padresob hoppez Cristianoil uai ti cah
peten Yucatan lae lai u kabaobe Fr. Juan de la
Puerta y Fr. Luis de Villarpando y Fr. Diego de
Becal y Fr. Juan de Guerrero y Fr. Merchol de
Benavente layob hoppes Cristianoil uai ti peten
chikin lae ti mato tac Cristianoil uai Cupul; pachal
hom to tac Cristianoil, baito bin cantic, ca bin
hoppoc toon uai ti Cupule.

22. 1546 años, lai hab ca uchi ahetzil [1] lae altose la tierra: 9 de Noviembre bol ulo de pasen 4 meses ca uchi tu bolonpis u kinil noviembre ti yabil de 1546 años canppel u cinanil katun; lae ca zihi lae kuchi hunppel hab yalcab uinicob; ca tali u molicubaob tu caten ocol u cibal patan, ca zihi katune ulel u cibahob ahezobob tali chikin tabsic uinicob ca yutzcinah katun lae Etz Cunul *y* Ah Camal talob chikin he ɔul cimsabiobe catul mehen ɔulob u camzah palil Mena ti cimob Chamaxe, ppatal u cibahob; ca talob Saci tohyol tulacal ɔulob ca liki katun yokolob lae [2] tihi t tun u cimsabal; Ah Etz Camal Tipakan Ah Pakam tu cimilhi Surusano yokol Nicte; tumen u cahalobe hunppel akab hi u cimil ɔul tumen uinicob lae ko-han yooc *y* u kaboob, ca bini tu kinil katun ti akab ti cah tulacal.

23. 1547 años lai hab ca paxi u chem Exboxe Ecabe; ca bini Espanolesob bakzahticob u ɔahob katun yok Boxte Ecabe ual Ekboxil.

24. Lae 1548 años ulci padre Emitanyo Saci chumes [3] Cristianoil.

25. Lae 1550 años mol ci cah tulacal tabal tal Manii.

26. 1551 años ulci padre Guadian Fr. Fernando

---

[1] aheɔil.   [2] tiihil.   [3] chunbez.

Guererro Saci Sisal lai oces haa tu hol uinicob lai chunbezob cristianoil uay tu cuch eabal Saci tulacal, tal chikin Cheel, tali Ecab, tali Cusamil, tali ti xaman, tali ti nohol, xan lai chunmes[1] u pakal monisterio Saci Sisal.

27. Lae 1552 años lai hab cahciob padresob yokab cuchi; lai yabil ulcob ah canbesah *y* kayob uai Zisale, talob chikin laobi canbez u kayob missa y bisperas ti canto de organo *y* chul y cantolano ti hunkul ma ohelon uai cuchi.

Lae 1553 años lai hab ca uli Oidor D. Tomas Lopes uai tal lumil Yucatan lae tali Castella ca uli tu [2]chibil tumen ca noh ahau Rey ahtepal de Castilla u yanton tu kab Españolesob uaye, lai haues ca tocabal tumen Españolesob, laix haues u chi on pek, laix ti chunmes u yanhal batabob ti cahal cah, ca tu ɔa u barail, laix ti ɔai u takail patan xan oxppel u yocol patan ti Españolesob yub te cib uluum ixim choyche y sulbiltab *y* yic, buul, yib cuum, xamach, ppuul, ca muc yoklal patan ta c yumil ɔulil c beta ti matac oidor ɔaic u nucul bahunbal; lai uchci u chabal kul chuuc tumen AhMacan Pech ca lukon Sisal yoklal u katci ah chucil kulchuc, lae tumen lai toci u chucil Ah Ceh Pech uay Cupul, lae lai talic uai tu pach Ah kin

---

[1] chunbez.   [2] chabil.

Pech Macan Pech u palil Ahmacan Pech yetel u nacomob ti cab Yaxkukul lae.

28. De 1519 años lai hab ca uli Españolesob uai tac cahal Con ah Ytza uai ti lum Yucatan, lae lai tin chicilbesah u kinil, yuil *y* yabil yan canal, Cen Dⁿ Pablo Pech, u mehen en Dⁿ Martin Pech, ti Xulcum Cheel, concixtadoren, uai lae Maxtunil yetel Chac Xulub Chen, tal kamah ix ɔulob tu uolol ca puczikal, maix ca ɔaab katun yah tiob laob lae Dⁿ Juan de Montejo Adelantado y u chayanil capi-tanob bay yanil u kabaob ti libro; ton ix yax kamah Cristianoil concixtadores Dⁿ Martin Pech u mehen Dⁿ Fernando Pech, Dⁿ Pablo Pech u mehen en Dⁿ Martin Pech, hel tu yoxlahunpis u kinil u de Octubre de 1518, ocic ha tu holob in mektan cahilob ti hunmolhob Maxtunile, ti ocol ha tu polob tumen yax obispo Dⁿ Franᶜᵒ Toral ti Maya uinicob; ca ¹oha tu polob men ca yum obispo lae cat ²es sabi u uinbail santo tiob cahob tulacal u uinbail S. Pedro *y* S. Pablo y S. Juan, y S. Luis *y* S. Antonio *y* S. Miguel *y* S. Francisco *y* S. Alonso y S. Agustin y S. Sebastian y S. Diego, ca u ³ɔibotahob oleos ca u kabatah Pᵒ yan cha oleos.

29. Lay u kahlail tulacal lae tin hun molcinzah

¹ ociha.   ² ezabil.   ³ ɔiboltahob.

uay ti librose uchebal u nuctic uba uinicob himac
bin oltic yohelto u ɔoc lukanil yanomal ca noh
ahau Dios uchac tumen tusinile.—U patanil hibic
ulci Espańolesob uay tac lumil lae tumen u yolat
ca yumil ti Dios ahtepal uay ti peten ; lae baix u
than ca yum Seńor Dⁿ Juan de Montejo y D.
Francᵒ de Monte lay yax ulob uai tac lumil lae
laix tu ɔah u thanil u cumtal iglesia ti ɔucenɔucil
cahob u hol cababob y yotoch cah u kuna ca yum
noh ahau bay u cah mensone u yotoch ah na mul-
beobe ¹.

30. Bay xan cu yalic ca noh yum Ah Naum
Pech Dⁿ Francᵒ de Montejo Pech y Dⁿ Juan Pech
lai u kabaob ca oci haa tu holob tumen padresob
y adelantado lay capitan hi layob ulob uai ti lume
Yocolpeten, hek lai kabanzabi ti Yucatanil tumen
ca yax yumob Espańolesob lae baix bin u patcantic
ca yum Espańolesob, hebic u beltahob, caxtu yalah
binil hunkul cuxlacon tumen Dios, caix ti yubah
Maya uinicob heklay u kabaob lae, ca tu yalah
Naum Pech ti u mektan cahil ti ɔuɔucencil:—
"Oheltex, talel u cah hunabku, ti peten heklai
hahal Diose, u chicul hahal Dios ; binex cuxlac, ca
cici kamex, ma a ɔaicex katun yokolob ca pas ma
u hanalob y yukalob ixim, cax, uluum, cab, buul u

---

¹ mulbaobe.

hanalob yoklal ¹u colcah ti Cristianoil lai u palil ton Dios;" bay tun cibahob mamac ɔai katun caix tu likzahubaob ca bin u yan teob Españolesob tu concixtob tu yet xinbal tahob ɔulob.

31. Bay xan he Nachi Cocom ti cahan tu holcacab Sutuytae tu chuccabal Chicħen Ytzae heklay kabansabi Chicħen Ytzaile he Ah Cohuot Cocome tu yantah u than Dios *y* ca noh ahau tu luksah u ²ponob u banderasob, utia ca noh ahau utial conquixta *y* adelantado *y* yum padre clerigo tu cuch cahil xan maix u ɔa yah katun u lukzahubaob ichilob kaxahob kunal *y* yotoch cah tu cuchteelob.

32. Hex Naɔi Mabun Chane culhi tu ca cabil u natatah bicil talel u cah hunkul cuxtal yoltah u kububaob ti Dios tu hahil Ah Catzimob *y* AhChulimob tu chuccabil Manil, *y* Ah Tutul Yiu hex uay ti lakin Chel *y* Tan Cupulob hex ti Campeche Naɔacab Canul; bay ɔa lukanhi u tan hahil Dios uay ti peten uay tu lumil Sacuholpatal Sacmutix tun, Ah Mutule, Tunal Pech culhi uay ti cah lae.

33. He Ah Naum Peche uay u payahe mehenob caix ti yalah:—"Oheltex, hun ynix u kaba kin ahbalcab bin uluk ahlikin cabob hun mexob Ahpul tu chicul hunabku ti peten ca xicex ti kam

---

¹ ocol cah.   ² panob.

bu hahil asilex[1]:" bay tan binciob tu xinbalob yalan che yalan haban, ca kuchiob tu tancabal Naɔay-
cab Canule Campech, ca yalahob:—"Hele tac u
yulel a uula, Ah Naɔacab Canule, caxti kam tuzebal la umen;" yalab lae ca tipp u chemob tu hol
u kaknabil Campech, caix ti[2] yalahob ca yumtah
banderasob sasacpon, ca ulon pixtahob Adelantado
caix katabitiob tumen lai Cristianoob Adelantado
uatub ocahalob ichil Castellano than, matan u natob ca uchen nucahob than:— "matan c ubah
than;" ci u thanob caix alabi Yucatanilob uay tu
lumil cutz tu lumil ceh.

34. Bay tun binciob capitanesob *y* ca yum Adelantado D[n] Fran[co] de Montejo lay tu beltah u yabal ppis *y* kuuch utial muse utial bucoh ɔimin[3] tumen binel u cibahob tu cahal Manii yicnal Ahtutul Xiu: ca kuchob Yiba caniob Yibae, kuchob
Nohcacab likul tal Becal, bay tun manciob Españolesob ca kuchob Mani yicnal Tutul Xiu caix ti
uacuntabic nacon Ikeb nacon Caixicum nacon Chuc
lay bin xic u paye Ah Cuat Cocom; lay tun u chun
u culcintabal [4] ahactan ob tumen u cuchulob ca
lukzabi u uichob yalan nohoch [5] yacatun sa bin tal
pulbil huntul lay ma lukzabi u uich ti yacatun

---

[1] a—ciil—ex.   [2] yilahob.   [3] tzimin.

[4] ahactunob.   [5] actunzabin.

sabin, luksabi u uich ca ɔa be ti ca bin nacpalancal ti yicnal Adelantado Manii, caix ualkahi
yah pululob tu cahal Cuuat Cocom; catun liki
Ah Naum Pech *y* tu catulilob xic u talez Ah
Cuat Cocom; cu kuchulob, ca yalah ti Naun Pech
bicil ma yilahi maix yabahi ca yalah bicil ti binan
tu Chicħen Ytzae tuzebal tal ci tu cail tumen
Ahpechob, ca kuchob Manil kube u cħasahob tu-
sebal u yalci Ah Cocom ma yilah bal uch tu cahal
caix ɔab u chucil ti cabin u chucob mac u beltah-
lobe.

35. Baix tun tal ci Ahpech tu cahalob yila u mektan
cahilob uinicilobe baytun talciob hex cat tal ɔulob
tumen bin uchci u cimsabal ɔuul ti cah tumen u
cuchulob, catun manobca biniob yicnal Ah Batun
Pech Cay Chel, lay tun yilahobe ca manob ca binob
Maxtunil yicnal Machi May *y* tun Ah Macan Pech;
bai tun ualkahciob tu lumilob tu mektan cahilob
tu Yaxkukule; lai Dⁿ Pablo Pech Ah Macan
Cam Pech tumenel halach uinic lai mektanmail
tulacal lai uay ti chi kin lae yoklal maix u lukul
yol nacomob, tulacal bayxan lay tumen culcinaben
in canant lay cacab Cħac Xubub Cħen lae tumenel
maseneal uinicob lae tan u ¹sa uinolabob lai tumen
²chic u nakci u yolah Dios ti cahob.

¹ ɔa uinalalob.   ² chiic.

36. Lae hex lay ytoria lae tulacal tux manel Sᵣ Españolesob *y* kubabaob yax padresob, *y* u kaba yax ɔulob bin ɔoloc ¹ tumen lai u ɔilibal, lae yoklal mentahan utial yoheltabal bic uchic concixta, uabic numya tu mansahob uay yalan chee yalan aak yalan haban, ichil lay hab lae *y* u cha yan yax uin-icob mehentzilob hancabob yoklal manal cappel oxppel hab cahanob ta muktun u ɔablahal cahob tumen ca yumil ɔulilob, laeta muktun u ppizil cahob u ppizil u kaxilob cahob tumen Oidor Tomas Lopes yan sedula tu kabob tumen ca noh Ahau utial tun xotlahal kaxob ti mac cu cahtalob, ti ma yanac cahob cuchi tumen te zihnalon be nae tulacalob, ti cu halach uinicil Naum Pech cuchi, ti ma uluc ɔulob heɔic Cristianoil uay ti lum cuchi, he tun cat kuchi u kinil u yulah uay ti peten, lae cat ul ɔulob uai ti lum Yucatan lae, ca binon kameob tumen u zahacil ca puczikal, cat ɔoci Cristianoil uay ti lum lae cat ɔablahon canante cacabob, ti ma yanac Sᵃ Yglesia cuchi, cat hau u cahil lay bena lae ma cah.

37. Helelae lay u chun in patcantic hen cex bin uchic u yuchul concixta bahun numya t mansah *y* Sᵣ Españolesob yoklal maya uinicob cuchi matan yolte ukuubaob ti Dios, ten tun cen D. Pablo Pech tin tzolah u xicinob ti cacab Maxtunil.

¹ tzoloc.

38. Bay tan matan culhani catun emon ti cacab
Chac Xulub Chen, ɔoci tun u Cumtal Sᵃ iglesia, lae
ca tun ppisah ca ppisbi tu ɔutpach cahlahbal yanumal
in mehenob u chen cimic yokolcab, tumen ma u
macan tu baltiob[1] tumen Maya uinicob, ma u manbal cuntabalob u chinal hen cex bax tu ɔahton ca
yumil ti Dios tumen u zahacil puczikale, lay tumen
ɔab u chucil ton tumen ca noh ahau Rey Ahtepal
y catun cumcintah Sᵃ iglesia utial kultic ca yumil ti
Dios *y* yotoch cah tu lakin iglesia u kuna ca noh
Ahau yetel meson.

39. Bay xan licix in betic in uotoch pakil na tu
xaman iglesia; ma u yalic Maya uinicob ua utialtob
tu kinil, lay tumen ci chicilbezic hebix in mentah
mailobe *y* yum Dⁿ Pablo Pech Ah Macan Pech, y
in yum Dⁿ Martin Pech Ah kom Pech, *y* in yum Dⁿ
Ambrosio Pech Op Pech ix u Maya kaba y Yxkil
Ytzam Pech y Dⁿ Estevan Pech Ahkulul Pech.

40. Tac kamah u noh comisionil u ppiz kaxob,
tu ɔah u licenciail ca noh Ahau Rey ahtepal ti ca
yumil yax Oidor Tomas Lopes utial ca u ɔa nucte
u than ton utial ca ppizic u pach ca tocoynail he
tux cahantacob uay uay tu pach cahal utial ca
utzac oheltic tux cu manel u ppizil ca luumil utial
kilacabob utial u tzenticubaob u ɔaic u hanalob ca

[1] beltahob.

encomenderosob, lay oklal cin ɔaic u juramentoil
tu tanil tulacal uinicob lay informacion lae u hahil
cu yilicob u tocoynailob tu xma yocol u yanal tocoynail, lay oklal ɔaic u hahil.

41. Heix macx yax encomendero uay ti caçab
Chaac Xulub Chen lae Dⁿ Julian Donsel encomendero hi uay ti cacah lae ca tu yalah ti batab caxi-
cob u ɔabob u chicul chi kax u luumob uay tu pach
u mektan cahil; yoklal tan u ppizil u chi lumob u
chi kaxob ti lakin, ti nohol, ti chikin, tulacal hen
cex max cu cahtalob, tumen ɔoctun u heɔel Cristianoil uay ti lume Chaac Xulub Cheen, y lix caci-
lech u yum Santiago patron ah canan cah utial
Dⁿ Pablo Pech.

1. The fifth division of the 11th Ahau Katun was placed when the Spaniards arrived and settled the city of Merida; it was during the 9th Ahau that Christianity was introduced; the year in which first came our lords the Spaniards here to this land was the

year 1511.

2. I, who am Nakuk Pech, of the first hidalgos conquistadores here in this land in the district Maxtunil, I am placed in the first town in the district Chac Xulub Chen. As thus it is given me to guard by my lord Ah Naum Pech, I wish to compose carefully the history and chronicle of the district of Chac Xulub Chen here, my first command, the town having two districts, Chichinica and, here, Chac Xulub Chen.

3. My name was Nakuk Pech before I was baptized, son of Ah Kom Pech, Don Martin Pech, of the town of Xul Kum Chel; thus we were given the districts to guard by our lord Ah Naum Pech from the town Mutul, and I was promoted to guard the district Chac Xulub Chen; when our

lords, the Spaniards, did not pass nor come here
to this land Yucatan, I was then governor here in
this town, here in this land, Chac Xulub Chen.
When our lord, the Señor Adelantado came here
to this province in the year 1519, I was head chief;
when the Spaniards came here to the land of
Maxtunil we received them with loving attention;
we also first gave them tribute and respect, and
then we gave to eat to the Spanish captains; he
who was called Adelantado came here to Maxtunil to the dwelling of Nachi May; then we went
to see that they should be given pleasures; they
did not even enter the towns, not even visited
the towns; they were here in this land for three
months, being placed here in the district of Maxtunil; then they departed and went to begin a
seaport, the seaport Ɔilam, and remained there
three years and a half.

4. They were there when my father went to make
delivery to them; he called the Adelantado returned here to this land; the maid servant named
Ixkakuk was presented to them by my father to
give them food and wait upon them; and they
were there when they were attacked by the
Cupuls; and they departed, and went to live at
Ecab Kantanenkin, as is called the land where

o

they settled; they were there when they were attacked by those of Ecab, and they departed and arrived at Cauaca, which they entered, and passed to the town Ɔekom, as the town is called; they passed it and arrived at the town Tixcuumcuuc, so-called;' and they departed from there and arrived at the town called Tinuum; and then they all set out in search of Chichen Itza, so-called; there they asked the King of the town to meet them, and the people said to them; "There is a King, O Lord," they said, "there is a King, Cocom Aun Pech, King Pech, Namox Chel, King Chel, of Ɔiɔantun; foreign warrior, rest in these houses," they said to them, by the Captain Cupul. They departed from Chichen Itza and arrived with King Ixcuat Cocom of Ake; "Lords, you cannot go, you will lose yourselves," was said to them by the King Ixcuat Cocom, and they turned back again, and went and arrived at Cauaca for the second time, and they reached the seaport called Catzun, where they marched by the sea, and went and returned to Ɔelebnae, as it is called, where they first settled when they first came to this land.

5. They remained in Chanpatun six years, when they went forth to Campeche; he, called the Adelantado, the first Spaniard, passed here to this

land; they were at Campeche when they asked tribute; according to orders by the chiefs to all the villages there was tribute. They passed on by the sea (asking) for tribute to be brought to them. Then I went with my companions Ah Macan Pech and his younger brother Ixkil Ytzam Pech, the king of the town Cumkal, and my father, who was in the town Xulcumcheel; these were my companions when I went back for the tribute; they saw it; also Nachi May accompanied us, because he knew that he (the Adelantado), did not know the language; because they first stayed at his house when they came, and for this reason they spoke to him to accompany them when they went after the tribute, because he was a friend to the Spaniards when it (the tribute) was delivered to the captains; from them we received coats and cloaks and shoes and rosaries and hats, and had much pleasure from the captains; we left when the Spaniards had ended giving these gifts; already we had our clothes when we arrived, the coats and cloaks (we) Ixkil Ytzam Pech of Conkal, our companions Ah Macan Pech of YaxKukul, and my father Ah Kom Pech, who were the greatest of us.

6. And I Nakuk Pech by name was head chief when they first delivered tribute, when we went to

Campech to deliver tribute, and we came back
when the Spaniards coming on the road from Campech came to the towns to dwell at Ichcanzihoo,
the city of Merida; and when it was heard that
the Spaniards were coming on the road from Campech we went to give them gifts, and I went the
second time to deliver tribute. And I Nakuk Pech
of this district of Chac Xulub Chen, and Ah Ma-
com Pech of the district Yan Kukul, and Ixkil
Ytzam Pech the head chief of Conkal, and also I
Nakuk Pech, chief here in the town Chac Xulub
Chen, entered into giving gifts to them a second
time at ꜫibikal, and they wished an abundance a
second time, and they were given gifts, pheasants,
and honey, and sweet food at ꜫibilkal, when they
came to settle at Merida; Don Francisco de Montejo, first Captain General, first came here to this
land, to Merida, with Don Francisco de Bracamonte and Francisco Tamayo and Juan de Pacheco and Perarberes; these captains came in the
year 1541.

7. In the year when these captains who commanded came to Merida to settle, then I, Ix Nakuk Pech, was chief, and when the Spaniards came
to Merida, I paid tribute to the conquerors at
Merida, as I was then chief here in the district

Chac Xulub Chen, Roderigo Alvarez being Secretary in the year 1542.

8. When the Adelantado made the distribution of towns to the conquerors by the captains, and the Secretary Roderigo Alvarez wrote out the list of tributes according to each division of the towns, all my companions and kinsmen paid tribute, sufficient tribute according to the division of tribute to the Spaniards which the Adelantado made by the captains, and the Secretary Roderigo Alvarez, in the first year the Spaniards came to Merida ; and I, Nakuk Pech, was taken and given to Don Julian Doncel the Encomendero, the first lord of the town Chac Xulub Chen, the first Encomendero, and my hand was given him by the captain Don Francisco de Montejo, and I was given for a chief to Don Julian Doncel, in his hand, and I began to take tribute for the holy fathers.

9. And I, Nakuk Pech, was thus chief when Alvarez, the first Alcalde Mayor, came to this province Yucatan, to Merida, and when Alvara de Carvayor was Alcalde Mayor; and when the Auditor Thomas Lopez came I was chief, and I was called Ix Nakuk Pech, and when I entered the water and received baptism, I was called Don Pablo Pech ; and I ceased to be called Nakuk Pech ; we first

chiefs were created hidalgos by the captains when possession was first taken of this province, and we first paid tribute to the foreigners, and possession was given to us by God and the ruling king; and our descendants are hidalgos, and all our sons, until the time shall come when the world shall end; and we chiefs were rulers in this land when there was no Holy Church in the districts, and before the Spaniards began to march over the country, or to congregate together in order to worship; and formerly, when the men were not Christians, I ruled wholly the men, and when I received Christianity I, Nakuk Pech, I was a chief; and I received the Holy Oils and the Holy Faith in order that I might teach it to all my subjects; and I was also the first to receive the rod of the justicia, because I went to aid the Word of God and our great Lord the ruling king; then our Lord, the Auditor Don Thomas Lopez, was the first who divided the tribute of the chiefs according to the towns they occupied; and when the tribute was satisfactorily finished by the governorship of the Auditor Don Thomas Lopez, I gave my rod to my son Don Pedro Pech, in the year 1552.

10. This was the number of the year when I received the rod from my father, Nakuk Pech,

Don Pablo Pech and of Ursula Pech, here in this town of Chac Xulub Chen, to serve God and our great ruler, the reigning king, in order that I may govern the town at this place Chac Xulub Chen.

11. The first descendants of Macan Pech and of Ah Kom Pech, of Xulkum Chel, came to their towns with their priests and chiefs, to the town of Yaxkukul, to Xulkum Chel and to Maxtunil ; they came back with their companions to this town ; they came also with their priests and chiefs and ministers back to their rulers, when they came to the town Yaxkukul; and we, also, when we arrived at this town of Chac Xulub Chen. When we settled here they appointed me, Nakuk Pech, by my father, Ah Kom Pech, son of Ah Tunal Pech, first descendant of Maxtunil, to govern this town.

12. When the Spaniards came to the towns of this land there were no Indians who had a will to pay tribute to the first Spaniards ; therefore the first Spaniards made an account of what towns were to be given to be governed. I, Nakuk Pech, I first received the town here, in the district Chac Xulub Chen, when first they came with orders to take it, with the chiefs, and captains and priests, whose names are Ah Kul Matu and (Ah) Kul Che ; and the first priests arrived, the priest Cocom,

the priest Tacu; and the captains arrived, the captain Nachan Cen and the captain Xuluc, as their names were, the captains who commanded when they came to this land Maxtunil, with the priest Chuc and his captains, to take possession; thus they found the town here, Chac Xulub Chen, when came the soldiers and ensigns, Ensign Kan, Ensign Xuluc, Ensign Pot, Ensign May, Ensign Ek, such were the names of the ensigns, the names of those I commanded as chief when I, Nakuk Pech, came to this town Chac Xulub Chen; thus my mind was strengthened when these things happened, and when I came here to settle here in the land and district Chac Xulub Chen.

13. I, Nakuk Pech, came here by (order of) the governor that I should strengthen the town Chac Xulub Chen; then among old men there was no sign that the Spaniards would come here to this land, nor was the village of Chac Xulub Chen strengthened then; it was when they heard the account, when the Spaniards came to the city of Merida and Christianity was received by the men of the province of Ceh Pech. I finished by gathering together all the town of Chac Xulub Chen, I, Don Pablo Pech, and my father, Don Martin Pech, Conquistador of Xulkum Cheel.

14. When the war against the Spaniards began
we spread out our forces together with them, and
went with my father, Ah Macan Pech, of the
first lineage of Yaxkukul, and Ixkil Yɔam Pech, of
the first lineage of Cumkal, and I went after them
to the war; then began the obligation of tribute to
our rulers for the Spanish governors in the town ;
when we went to the war there was *pinole* and *tuce*
to drink, because they were disgusted with the
Christians ; for six months we and my companions followed the Christians in their misfortunes ;
my father was then governed by the regidors, who
saw that all that I write in my information truly
happened, everything, in order that it may be
known by my family, my sons, in the hereafter,
until the end of the world, for my title and evidence given me by our Lord God and our great
lord, the reigning king; I have no tribute nor do
I pay tribute, nor will my sons nor my daughters
pay tribute, because our Lord God released me
from it in the fear of my heart; before I had seen
the face of the Spaniards I had been given willing-
ness that I should deliver myself and all my town
into the hands of the Spaniards, in order that they
might be inhabited by the captains, the Adelantado
and the first conquistadores who came here to this

land, Yucatan; and the year the first foreigners came here to the land of the Cupuls was the year 1511.

15. In former times no one saw Spanish foreigners, not until Jeronimo de Aguilar was captured by the natives of Cozumel; then first the whole of the country became known, because all the country was marched over; but because the whole of the land was not made use of I spoke of it before the king, when there went before the king Ah Macan Pech, Don Pedro Pech, and his followers, and the first of his lineage, and all his chiefs after him; they went after him to honor the king, that he might see the faces of his servants; then fifty of the principal men went afterwards to the lord the ruling king, to obey him at table, far off in Spain, and those remained to obey before the ruling King; then the ruler said that all should pay tribute and all their sons, even we the Pechs of the first lineage in this land, and the first lineage of the Cupuls; then it was said, there is a great province, and many men and things in the land, and an account shall be made of it before our great king, and now they shall come to fix the limits of the land for our beloved king. Thus the land was discovered by Aguilar, who was eaten by

Ah Naum Ah Pat at Cuzamil in the year 1517. In this year the katun ended, and then ended the placing of the town stone, for at each twentieth stone they came to place the town stones, formerly, when the Spaniards had not yet come to Cuzamil, to this land; since the Spaniards came, it has ceased to be done.

16. In the year 1519 first came the Spaniards here to Cuzamil, for the third time, Fernando de Cortes and Espoblaco Lara. On the 28th of February, there came to Cuzamil for the first time those who knew to speak the true words. In this year the eaters of anonas first arrived at Chichen, and then for the first time Chichen Itza became known to the great Spaniards, (and) to Don Francisco de Montejo, Adelantado, the governor, when they were posted at Chichen Ytza.

17. In the year 1521, on the 13th day of August, the territory of Mexico was taken by the Spaniards. The third attack on the same Spaniards took place by all the towns here in the town of Cupul, when they asked Ah Ceh Pech about the killing at Zalibna, and his companion-king Cen Pot of Tixkokhoch of the province of Ticanto, with the priest Ich Kak Mo of Itzmal the companion of Holtun Ake. The year in which the Span-

iards arrived at Chichen Itza for the second time to settle at Chichen Itza was that when arrived the captain Don Francisco de Montejo, the just one, leader of the Cupuls. They arrived at the town twenty years after they arrived at Chichen Ytza (the first time), where they were called eaters of anonas, biters of anonas.

18. In the year 1542, the Spaniards settled the territory of Merida; the first speaker, the companion priest Kinich Kakmo and the king of the Tutulxiu of the capital Mani humbled their heads, and the first families were settled; then first they came under tribute the third time (the Spaniards) came to this land, and they established themselves permanently, and stopped here. The first time when they came here to Chichen Itza they began to eat anonas; never before had anonas been eaten, and when the Spaniards ate them they were called anona-eaters; the second time they came to Chichen they stopped at the house of the Captain Cupul; the third time they arrived they settled permanently, in the year 1542 they settled permanently in the territory of Merida, the 13th Kan being the year-bearer, according to the Maya reckoning.

19. In the year 1543 the Spaniards went north of the Chels to procure Maya men for servants

because there were no men for servants at Merida ; they came to procure men for servants for
their bidding ; when they reached Popce the tribute was increased by those from Merida, when
those who command arrived at Popce, and they
went on to Tikom, and the Spaniards remained at
that time in Tikom more than twenty days before
they departed.

20. In the year 1544 the Spanish Captain Asiesa was posted in Cauaca, and the chiefs were gathered together from Cauaca for the tribute, and
they gave in Cauca honey, pheasants and maize ;
then they placed in prison the priest Caamal from
Sisal, and asked for an account of all the towns ;
one year he was kept by them in prison ; he then
served as guide to the Spaniards when they came
to Valladolid, and this priest Kamal of Sisal entered as chief at Valladolid, and was called Don
Juan Caamal de la Cruz, because he spoke very
truthfully ; he first introduced the cross in Cauaca,
and he was listened to by the Spaniards, and for
this he entered as chief at Sisal, and being chief a
long time he died.   He was also guide to the Spaniards when they went to war with Tixkochnah ;
and when the Spaniards had been posted one year
in Cauaca, they went forth and came to Vallado-

lid on purpose to see the men the chief Kamal had placed in prison.

21. In the year 1545 the Spaniards were posted at Valladolid, and in this year Christianity began by the fathers of the order of San Francisco in the port of Champoton; there first came the fathers having in their hands the Redeemer Jesus Christ by name, that they might teach the serving men; and first they came to the port of Champutun to the west of this province called here Ichcansiho, then to Merida, the town Ichcansiho as it is called. These are the names of the fathers who began Christianity in this country Yucatan, Fr. Juan de la Puerta, and Fr. Luis de Villarpando, and Fr. Diego de Becal, and Fr. Juan de Guerrero, and Fr. Merchol de Benavente, these began Christianity in the west of this country, before Christianity came here to Cupul; afterwards the trumpet of Christianity came here, as I was saying, and it began here at Cupul.

22. In the year 1546 there was a conjuration in the highlands of the country; on the 9th of November there had been peace for four months, and it occurred on the 9th day of November of the year 1546 that there was war after four months: it began and continued for one

year among the men, when they were gathered together for the second time for the tribute of wax; when the war began it took place that the conjurors came from the west to deceive the people and to set in order the war; the conjuror Cunul and Ah Camal came from the west and killed the Spaniards and two sons of the Spaniards, scholars at Mena; they died at Chamax, where they wished to remain; then came to Valladolid all the Spaniards who were well when the war broke out, and then began the massacre; the conjuror Camal Tipakan, of Pakam, killed Surusano over against Nicte; at the towns one night the Spaniards were slain because the people fell sick in their hands and feet; there was then for a day and a night war in all the towns.

23. In the year 1547 a ship was destroyed by Ex Box at Ecab; then the Spaniards went to make him fear, and made war against Box of Ecab, son of Ek Box.

24. In the year 1548 the father Ermitanyo came to Valladolid to begin Christianity.

25. In the year 1550 there was a general reunion of the towns and their dependencies at Mani.

26. In the year 1551 the father guardian, Fr.

Fernando Guerrero, came from Valladolid to Sisal and he baptized the people and introduced Christianity here into all the territory of Valladolid west of the Chels; they came from Ecab, they came from Cozumel, they came from the north, they came from the south, and also he began the building of the monastery Valladolid-Sisal.

27. In the year 1552 the fathers settled here; in this year they came to teach and sing here at Sisal, they came from the west to teach and sing mass vespers with the singing of the organ and flute, and the canto llano, which never before did we know here.

In the year 1553 the Auditor, Don Thomas Lopez arrived here in this land of Yucatan from Castilla, and he arrived as a messenger from our great ruler, the reigning king of Castilla, to protect us against the hand of the Spaniards here. He put a stop to our being burned by the Spaniards, he put a stop to our being bitten by dogs, he introduced the appointing of chiefs in each village by the giving of the baton; he also adjusted the tribute for the third time, the tribute introduced by the Spaniards, mantles, wax, pheasants, maize, buckets, salt, peppers, broad beans, narrow beans, jars, pots, vases, all for tribute to our Spanish rulers, which we paid before the Auditor had given his attention to these things. At this time occurred the capture of the priest Chuuc by Ah Macan Pech when we left Sisal, because he wished the priest Chuc to be captured, as he had prevented the capture of Ah Ceh Pech here in Cupul; afterwards the priest Pech, Macan Pech with the servants of Macan Pech and his captains, came here to this town of Yaxkukul.

28. From the year 1519 when the Spaniards came here to the town of Conah Itza, here in this land, Yucatan, I have set forth the days, the months and the years as above stated, I, Don Pablo Pech, the son of Don Martin Pech of Xul Kum Cheel, conquistador, here at Maxtunil and Chac Xulub Chen; since we received the Spaniards with good will and heart, nor did we make war upon them, Don Juan de Montejo, Adelantado, and the rest of the captains, as their names are in the book; we also first received Christianity, we the conquistadores, Don Martin son of Don Fernando Pech, Don Pablo Pech son of Don Martin Pech, on the 13th day of the month of October, 1518; all my subjects received baptism in Maxtunil; they were baptized by the first bishop to the Maya people, Don Francisco Toral; and when he baptized us

P

our father the bishop showed the images of the saints to all the villages, images of Saint Peter and St. Paul, and St. John and St. Louis, and St. Antony, and St. Michael, and St. Francis, and St. Alonzo, and St. Augustin and St. Sebastian, and St. Diego; and they desired the oils, and he who was called Peter took the oils.

29. Such is the chronicle of everything I have collected for the books, in order that the people might know it, whoever wished to know it, as had decreed it from the beginning our great lord God who governs the universe. It is the declaration of how the Spaniards came to this land, here to this country; by the will of the lord, the ruling God, also by the orders of our lord Don Juan de Montejo, and Don Francisco de Montejo, who first came here to this land, and gave orders that churches should be built in the plastered villages, in the outlying districts, and a town house and a temple for our great ruler, and also a public house for travelers.

30. Thus also said our great father, Ah Naum Pech, Don Francisco de Montejo Pech, and Don Juan Pech, as were their names when they were baptized by the fathers; and as the Adelantado, the Captain, those who came here to this land Yocol Peten, but called Yucatan by the first

Spaniards, as they the Spaniards, clearly relate. When our lord the Spaniards said that we are to live eternally with God, and when the Maya men heard the names, then spoke Naum Pech to those he commanded, with suavity:—"Know ye, there comes to the town the one God, to the country the true God, the sign of the true God; go ye to live with Him, joyfully receive Him, do not war against Him, and if they have not to eat or drink give them maize, fowls, pheasants, honey, beans to eat, that Christianity may enter and that we may be servants of God;" thus they wished it, and they did not make war, but rose up and went to aid the Spaniards in the conquest and marched together with the foreigners.

31. Thus also Nachi Cocom, who dwelt in the chief town of Zututa in the province Chichen Itza, that called Chichen Itza, and Ah Cahuot Cocom, aiding the word of God and our great King, delivered up their standards and banners for the sake of our great King, for the conquest, and received the Adelantado and the father the priest in their towns, nor did they make war, but abstained from all injury, and laid out churches and town-houses for their followers.

32. And Naoi Mabun Chan settled in the district,

and understood that the eternal life had come to
his village, and wished that to God truly would be
delivered the Catzins and Chuls in the district of
Mani, and the Tutulxiu, and the Chels in the East,
and the (middle) Tan Cupuls and in Campeche Naɔacab Canul; thus this earth was given by God to
be redeemed, this land Zacuholpatal Zacmutixtun;
and Tunal Pech of Mutul settled here in this town.

33. And Ah Naum Pech called the youths and
said to him — "Know ye, that on the day called 1
Ymix it will dawn, there will come from the eastern
lands bearded men with the sign of the only God
to this land; go to receive them with true pleasure;" therefore they went and marched under the
trees, under the branches, and they arrived at the
house of Naɔay Cab, of Canul at Campech and
said :—" He, your guest, is now coming, Ah Naɔa
Cab of Canul, receive him promptly." Thus they
said when the ships appeared in the port of Campeche,when they saw the banners waving, the white
standard, and they came, when he had cast anchor,
to the Adelantado, and were asked in Castilian by
the Christians, and the Adelantado, whether they
had been baptized; but they did not know his language, and replied : "We do not understand the
words ;" so they said, and thus they named this

land here Yucatan, (which was known to us as) the land of the wild turkey, the land of the deer.

34. Thus then the captains and our lord the Adelantado Don Francisco de Montejo went on; and they made much cloth and thread to cut into clothing for the horses, as they wished to go to the town of Mani, to the Tutulxiu. When they came to Yiba they held a talk in Yiba; they arrived at Nohcacab coming out of Becal; thus the Spaniards passed and arrived at Mani, to Tutulxiu, and then were appointed the chief Ikeb, the chief Caixicum and the chief Chuc to go to invite Ah Cuat Cocom. They were at first taken and placed in a cave by his followers: then their eyes were put out in that great cave of weasels, and there was not one who did not have his eyes put out in the cave of weasels; their eyes were put out and they were given the road to go groping to the Adelantado at Mani; and thus returned those who were cast out of the town of Cuat Cocom. Then Ah Naum Pech rose up with both of them and came to Ah Cuat Cocom; when they arrived, he said to Ah Naum Pech that he had not seen nor heard of it; he said he had gone to Chichen Itza, and he came promptly to the towns with the Pechs, and they arrived at Mani to deliver up promptly (the offenders);

and the Cocom said he had not witnessed what had happened in his village, and he would give permission that they should be taken who had done it.

35. Then Ah Pech came to the towns in order to see the people governed in them; the Spaniards also came, but on account of the massacre of the foreigners by the people, they passed on and went to Ah Batum Pech of Chel, whom they saw, and passed on, and went to Maxtunil, to Nachi May and Ah Macan Pech; they then returned to their lands to the towns they governed at Yaxkukul; Don Pablo Pech, Ah Macan Pech, was governor of all the district to the west, nor did his captains at all give up their spirits; soon I was appointed to guard the territory Chac Xulub Chen, because the serving men were at war on account of the labor given them, and by taking them the will of God was fulfilled in the towns.

36. Such is the complete history of how passed the Spaniards and how the first fathers were received, and the names of the first conquerors I shall set forth according to the register, because this is composed in order that it may be known how the conquest occurred, and in what manner they labored here, under the trees, under the branches

under the bushes, in those years and months; and
what the people and their sons found to eat; for
from two to three years they labored in the distribution of the towns, by our rulers the Spaniards;
they also labored in the measuring of the towns,
and the measuring of the forests of the towns
by the Auditor Tomas Lopez, holding in his hand
the Cedula of our great lord the king, that forests
should be cut by whoever settled. When there
were no towns we were natives here of official
houses, Naum Pech being governor of all, nor at
that time had the Spaniards come here to establish Christianity in this land; but when the day
came that their arrival took place, when the Spaniards came to this land Yucatan, we received them
with a friendly heart, and Christianity was introduced into this land, and we were appointed to
guard the villages, when as yet there was no
church; and now they have ceased building official
houses or villages.

37. Thus I began to relate how the conquest
took place and how many sufferings we under-
went with our lords, the Spaniards, from the
natives who were not willing to deliver themselves
to God; thus I recount what I heard concerning
the town Maxtunil.

38. We did not settle there, but descended to the town Chac Xulub Chen, and when the Holy Church was finished in Cumtal, we measured its sides and took possession so that our children should remain there from the beginning until the end of the world, so that the natives should not obstruct us, nor enchant by the throwing of stones anything which had been given us by God and our lord through the fear of our hearts; for this our great lord the ruling king gave us the authority; and when the church was prepared in which to worship our lord and God, and the public house to the east of the church and the temple of our great king and the residence.

39. I also built my house of stone to the north of the church. And that the natives may not in the future say that it belongs to them, for this I show forth the occurrences as I did them with my father, I, Don Pablo Pech, Ah Macan Pech, and my father Don Martin Pech, Ah Com Pech, my lord Señor Don Ambrosio Pech, his native name being Op Pech, and Ixil Yzam Pech, and Don Esteban Pech, Ah Culub Pech.

40. We received the royal commissions to measure the forests. The license was given by our great monarch the ruling king through our

lord the first auditor, Tomas Lopez, that he should give us years ago his order that the uncultivated fields should be measured wherever they are, here back of the town, that we may know where the boundaries of our lands pass in order that parents and children may maintain them and give food to the Encomenderos. Therefore I swear before the people that this information is true, that they may have it in sight so that no uncultivated field shall entrench upon another uncultivated field ; for this reason I set forth the truth.

41. The first Encomendero here in Chac Xulub Chen was Don Julian Doncel, who ordered the chiefs that they should go to place the marks of the limits of their forest lands here back of the towns they governed, and thus they were led to measure the boundaries of their lands and the forests toward the East, the South and the West, for the benefit of all who dwell therein ; because already Christianity was established in this land of Chac Xulub Chen with our holy lord Santiago the patron who guards the town of Don Pablo Pech.

NOTES.

1. "The fifth division of the 11th Ahau Katun was placed" (*i. e.* in the wall or in the Katun Stone), (see page 57, where this expression is explained). In other words, the first arrival of the Spaniards at Merida took place at the close of the 11th Ahau Katun. This was July, 1541, and it is in gratifying conformity with Bishop Landa, who also states that that month was the commencement of a 20-year period; but he says that at that date the 11th Katun began, while Pech goes on to say that it was the next in order, the 9th. (See Landa, *Relacion*, p. 314.)

Noh cah te ti Ho, the great town at Ho. This was the native name of the ancient city which stood on the present site of Merida, and, by the Mayas, is in use to this day. *Ho* is the numeral 5, and some have supposed that the name was given on account of five large mounds or buildings said to have been conspicuous in the ancient city. That there were precisely five is not positively stated by the old historians, though four are specified. This theory would suppose that the name was given to the city only after these large structures were completed, and that its name during that time had been lost. But this is not improbable.

In fact, the ancient name of Merida was not Ho, but *Ichcanzihoo*, as appears from a later passage in Pech's narrative and from numerous others in the Books of Chilan Balam. *Ho* is only the abbreviation of this long name. It ap-

pears to mean "The five (temples) of many serpents." *Can*
is the generic term for serpent, and *ich* used as a prefix denotes a place where there is an abundance of what the noun
means: thus *ichche* = a place where the trees are tall and dense;
ichxiu, a place where the grass is tall and thick (*Diccionario
de Motul*). The serpents were probably those sculptured in
stone or painted on the walls. This theory receives additional probability from an entry in the *Diccionario de Motul,* MS.,
which relates that the largest mound in ancient Merida, situated back of the present convent of San Francisco, was called
by the natives *ahchuncan,* and that this was the name of the
idol which used to be worshiped there. Its signification
would be "the first or primitive serpent," or "the first speaker," *i. e.* oracle, as *can* means both serpent and speech.

The temples at Ho were not in use when the Spaniards
arrived, nor had they been for many generations. Apparently
only a few huts of wood and straw made up the village, while
these vast ruins were even then covered to the summit with a
heavy growth of timber in all respects like the virgin forest
around them. This is clearly stated by the Friar Lorenzo
de Bienvenida, who came to Merida in 1545. I quote his
expressions from a letter to the King in 1548:—

"La ciudad esta la tierra adentro treinta y tres leguas;
llamase la *ciudad de Merida;* pusieronle asi por los edificios
superbos que hai en ella, que en todo lo descubierto en Indias
no se han hallado tan superbos edificios, de canteria bien
labrada, i grandes las piedras; no hai memoria de quien los
hizó; parecenos que se hicieron antes de la venida de Christo
porque tan grande estaba el monte encima dellos como en lo
bajo de la tierra; son altos de cinco estados de piedra seca i
encima los edificios, quatro quartos todo de celdas como de

Frailes, de veinte pies de luengo i de diez de ancho, i todas las portadas de una piedra, lo alto de la puerta i de boveda, i destos hai en la tierra otros muchos. Esta gente natural no habitaba en ellos, ni hacen casa sino de paja y madera, habiendo mas apareja de cal i piedra que en todo lo descubierto. En estos edificios tomamos sitio los Frailes para casa de San Francisco; lo que habia sido cultura de demonios, justo es que sea templo' donde se sirve à Dios, etc." (*Carta de Fr. Lorenzo de Bienvenida, 1548, MS.*)

The date, 1511, given as that of the first arrival of the Spaniards, refers to the shipwreck of Aguilar and his companions, who in that year were thrown on the eastern coast.

This introductory paragraph was entirely miscontrued by Avila, and nearly as much so by Brasseur. I add their translations to illustrate this.

Translation of Avila.

"A la quinta vez que sentó el noveno Rey en la guerra cuando llegaron los Españoles que se poblaron en la ciudad de Merida, el principal Rey de esa ciudad era siempre cacique y el año en que llegaron los Señores Españoles aqui en esta suelo fué el de 1511."

Translation of Brasseur.

"C'est à la cinquième division cimentée (dans le mur) de ce onzième Ahau-Katun qu'arrivèrent les Espagnols et qu'ils s'établirent à Ti-Uoh de ce pays de Ti-Ho, et c'est à la neuvième de cet Ahau que s'établit le Christianisme, cette année même que vinrent nos seigneurs les Espagnols en cette contrée, c'est à dire, en l'année 1511."

It will be seen that the former completely travesties the

passage, while the latter mistakes the proper names and destroys the chronological value of the dates given.

2. *Hidalgos conquistadoren*, Spanish titles which we are surprised to find a native claiming ; but later on (§ 9) he informs us that he was authorized to employ them by the Spanish officials.

Chichinica was a pueblo near Chicxulub, which is now no longer in existence.

3. *Ti ma ococ haa tin pol cuchi*, " formerly, when the water will not entered to my head " *i. e.*, before I was baptized. This complicated construction of the negative (*ma*), a future (*ococ* from *ocol*) and the sign of the past tense (*cuchi*), also occurs on an earlier page (98), where we have the sentence *uacppel haab u binel ma ɔococ u xocol oxlahun ahau cuchi*, six years before the end of the 13th ahau. *Ocol haa*, syncopated to *ocola*, and even *oca*, was the usual term for Christian baptism.

Xulkumcheel was a pueblo which does not seem to have survived.

Ah Naum Pech, likul tu cah Mutul. Ah Naum Pech from, or native of, the town Mutul. The latter is the modern Motul, about 22 miles easterly from Chicxulub. The name is also spelled Mutul by Cogolludo (*Historia de Yucatan*, Lib. VI, cap. VII).

Halach uinic, previously explained, was the ancient native title of chief of a village. It is the same word which Oviedo, in his report of Grijalva's expedition deforms into *calachini* (*Historia de las Indias*, Lib. XVII).

The date, 1519, like various others in the narrative, appears to have been erroneously entered or copied. It should probably be 1539. *Maxtunil* does not at present exist. ɔ*ilam* is a town north of Itzamal, near the sea coast. It is by some identified as the spot where Francisco de Montejo embarked after his retreat from Chichen Itza, in 1528.

4. The *Kupuls* were the family who reigned in the eastern province, where Valladolid was founded. They long retained their hostility to the Spaniards. *Ekab* was situated on the coast opposite the island of Cozumel. ɔ*ekom* should probably read Tekom. *Tixcuumcuuc* no longer exists. *Tinuum* is a town 4 leagues north of Valladolid, on the road to Itzamal. ɔ*i* ɔ*antun* is a town north of Itzamal, said by Sanchez Aguilar to have been the ancient capital of the princely house of the Chels. *Ake* is probably the modern ɔonataké. *Catzim* is now the name of a hacienda in the Department of Itzamal, some distance from the coast. ɔ*elebna* is unknown.

The expression *tumen naob Bon cupul*, translated by Avila "porque esa casa es de Bon Cupul," I think is an error of the copyist for *tumen nacon Cupul*. See also § 18.

5. *Hokzah uba*, they betook themselves. The termination *uba* is that of the third person of reflexive verbs.

Nachi May, already mentioned, was a member of an ancient princely house mentioned by Landa and Sanchez Aguilar. One of them, Ahkin May, was apparently the hereditary high priest. The effort has been made to derive from their name the word *Maya*, and Brasseur would carry us to Haiti in order to discover its meaning (Landa, *Relacion*, p. 42, note), but this is unnecessary. *May* in the Maya tongue means "a hoof," as of a deer, and is a proper name still in use. There is no reason to suppose it in any way connected with *Maya*.

Matanok I take to be an error for *matanon*, from *mat* (pret. *matnahi*).

6. Ɔ*ibikal* may be, as suggested by Dr. Berendt, Tipikal, a town in the district of Merida. There is another of the name in the Sierra Alta (*Estadistica de Yucatan*, 1814).

Francisco de Bracamonte is mentioned by Cogolludo as among the first settlers of Merida.

7. Cogolludo mentions Rodrigo Alvarez as "Escribano del juzgado," who came with Montejo (*Historia de Yucatan*, Lib. III, cap. VI, and elsewhere).

8. *U toxol cahob*, the distribution of the towns, literally " the pouring out ; " Avila translates it by "cuando se repartian los pueblos." The Spanish system of "repartimientos" and "encomiendas" was adopted in Yucatan,

9. The licentiate Alvares de Caravajal was alcalde mayor from 1554 to 1558. (Cogolludo, *Hist. de Yucatan*, Lib. V. cap. XV.)

10. This was apparently written by Don Pablo Pech, the son of the writer of the remainder of the history, and inserted in order to corroborate the statement just made by his father, that the latter had transferred the magistracy to him.

11. The *holpop*, literally "head of the mat," perhaps because when the company sat around or on the mat his place was at its head, was the official who had charge of the *tunkul* or wooden drum, with which public meetings, dances, summons to war, etc. were proclaimed, and with which the priests accompanied their voices in reciting the ancient chants (Cogolludo, *Hist. de Yucatan*, Lib. IV, cap. V). He was called *ahholpop*, and had charge of the public hall of the village, the *popolna*, "casa de comunidad," in which public business was transacted (*Diccionario de Motul*, MS.)

The *ahkulel* was the official second in command in a town or district. He acted in place of the *batab* or the *ahcuchcab*.

The verb *kulel* means to transact business for another, to act as deputy.

Ahkin was the ordinary word for priest in the old language; *kin*, sun, day, time; *ahkin*, he who was familiar with the days and times, with the calendar, and also with the past and the future.

12. *U chun u thanob;* the *chunthan* or *ahchunthan*, literally, he who has the first word, was the member of the village who took the leading part in matters of business. The office and name are still in existence in the native village communities of Yucatan. (See Garcia y Garcia, *Historia de la Guerra de Castas en Yucatan*, Introd., p. xli.)

The *ahkul* was an envoy or messenger, who carried the orders of the prince to his people and to foreign princes. The title was usually prefixed to the name of the person.

The *holcan*, "head caller," was a military official in each village, whose duty it was when war was announced to summon the men in his district capable of bearing arms (see Landa, *Relacion*, p. 174).   The Spanish writers translate it by *alferez*.

The *nacon* was an elective war chief, who held his position for the term of three years (Landa, *Relacion*, pp. 161, 173). The name is derived from *nacal*, to rise, go up, and hence as a delegate or elected representative (as is stated by the *Dicc. de Motul*).

13. The *nucteelob* were the *ancianos*, the wise old men of the village; *manak*, a trace or sign that appears at a distance and then disappears.   *U manak uinic ti ulah* = I saw the trace of a man to-day, but it is no longer visible.   *Diccionario de Motul, MS.*

" The province of Ceh Pech " was that in which Merida

was: "*u tzucub ahcehpechob*, la provincia de los Peches al lado de Motul y Cumkal." *Dicc. de Motul, MS.*

14. *Kah, pinole*, is a drink made by mixing the meal of roasted maize with water. The word *tuce* (or, it may be, *tuze*) I do not find in any dictionary, nor does Avila translate it. The passage is an obscure one. Avila renders it "cuando fuimos à la guerra, bebian piñole y *tuce*, porque estaban enojados con los Cristianos." Possibly these were two articles of food especially used on warlike raids.

U zahacil in puczical, a cant phrase probably borrowed from the missionaries = "the fear of my heart,"—in my humbleness. *Puczikal* appears to be a root-word, though of three syllables. It means the heart of men and animals, also the mind or soul, the desires, and the interior of certain growths, as the pith of maize, etc. (*Dicc. de Motul.*)

The year 1511 was that of the shipwreck of the deacon Geronimo de Aguilar and his companions, who were the first whites known to the natives of Yucatan.

The reference which is made in this section to a deputation of fifty natives to Spain, is not mentioned, so far as I remember, by other historians. As in some respects my translation differs from that of Avila, I give his.

" Cuando llegò ante el monarca Ahmacan Pech, Don Pedro Pech, y sus deudos, sus primeros descendientes, sus capitanes, todos fueron con el para honrar el monarca y vea la cara á sus vasallos indigenas, y escogió cincuenta de los grandes de ellos para llevar tras de el al monarca reinante para servirlos en la mesa alli lejos en España, pero los que vomitaron en el festejo delante del monarca reinante, esos entonces dijò el Rey que pagaron tributos todos y todos sus descendientes, mas nosotros los Peches," etc.

Q

The phrase *mac xenahi tu tzicile* Avila translates "who vomited at the feasts;" but I believe *xenhi*, vomited, is a misreading for *xanhi*, remained, and *tzicil* is obedience, as serving-men.

Lae te hantabi, who was eaten; Aguilar himself was not eaten, as he was rescued by Cortes, in 1519, and served him as interpreter. But some of his companions were eaten by the natives, not of Cozumel, but of the coast to the south, and this is what Pech meant to say, unless, indeed—and I am inclined to prefer this view—we read *hantezahbi* instead of *hantabi*, which would give the sense "the land was discovered by Aguilar, who was given food (supported, maintained) by Ah Naum," etc. For particulars about Aguilar see Herrera, *Hist. de las Indias*, Dec. II, Lib. IV, cap. VIII.

Lai yabil hauic, etc. This is an important sentence, as fixing a date in the ancient chronology. *U tunil balcah* is an ancient term, not explained in the dictionaries. *Balcah* (or *baalcah*) means "a town and the people who compose it" (Pio Perez, *Diccionario*), hence people, the world, as the French use *monde*. From many references in the Maya manuscripts I derive the impression that the last stone in the katun pillar was placed in turn by the towns, each giving its name to the stone and the cycle (see ante, p. 171).

Assuming the correctness of the figures 1517—and there is no reason to doubt it—then Pech counted the katuns as of 24 years each, as Pio Perez maintained was correct; because he has already informed us in his introductory paragraph that the year 1541 was the close of the 11th Ahau, and 1541 — 1517 = 24.

16. The two previous visits referred to were probably those of Cordova, 1517, and Grijalva, 1518. "Those who knew

to speak the true words," refers to the Catholic priests. All the historians of Cortes' expedition dwell on the effect produced on the natives of Cozumel by the religious services he held there.

The date, Feb. 28, 1519, seems correct, although it is not mentioned by any other writer I have at hand. Cortes left Havana, Feb. 19.

Lai yabil, "in this year," evidently a date is omitted, as the first arrival of the Spaniards at Chichen Itza was either at the close of 1526 or beginning of 1527. One of the Maya MSS. gives the year as *bulucil Muluc*, the 11th Muluc. The Maya year, it will be remembered, began on the 16th of July.

"It was on the memorable thirteenth of August, 1521, the day of St. Hippolytus, that Cortes led his warlike array for the last time across the black and blasted environs which lay around the Indian capital, etc." Prescott, *Conquest of Mexico*, Book VI, chap. VIII. There is little doubt but that the tidings of the dreadful destruction of the mighty Tenochtitlan was rapidly disseminated among the tribes far down into Yucatan and Central America, and made a profound impression on them.

This section is confused and difficult. Avila translates:—

"Fueron atacados por tercera vez los mismos Españoles por todos los pueblos aqui en el pueblo de Cupul cuando hallaron à Ah Ceh Pech muriendose en una casa no embarrada y à su compañero el otro Rey Cen Pot," etc.

18. The official date of the founding of the city of Merida was Jan. 6, 1542.

The anona or custard-apple does not seem to have been eaten by the natives, and it impressed them as strange and somewhat unnatural to witness the Spaniards suck them.

Ca u tocahob nao bon Cupul; this is translated by Señor Avila : "quemaron al capitan Cupul :" they burned the captain Cupul; but I take it to be a misreading for *ca u yotochob nacom Cupul,* and have so translated it. There is no account of a leader of the Cupuls having been burned, and, moreover, this is in accordance with § 4.

Another important chronological statement is made in this section, to wit, that the year 1542 (I suppose July 16, 1541– July 15, 1542 is meant) was 13 Kan. As Pech has already told us that it was also the first year of the 9th Ahau Katun, we have the date fixed in both methods of reckoning, that is, by the Kin Katun as well as the Ahau Katun, according to the calendar which his family used.

19. The town of Tikom is still in existence, but I have not been able to find Popce on any of the maps. The Chels were a well known princely family in ancient Yucatan. The *Dicc. de Motul* says their province was that of ɔizantun.

26. The Don Juan Caamal whose acts are briefly sketched in this section is the same mentioned in the *auto* given previously, page 117. It is still a family name in Yucatan (Berendt, *Nombres Proprios en lengua Maya*, folio. *MS.*)

21. The first mission to Yucatan was that of Fr. Jacobo de Testera, with some companions whose names have not been preserved, 1531 to 1534 (see Geronimo de Mendieta, *Historia Eclesiastica Indiana*, pp. 380, 665 ; Torquemada. *Monarquia Indiana*, Lib. IX, cap. XIII, Lib. XX, cap. XLVII). They were stationed at Champoton and did not penetrate the country. The next attempt was in 1537. Testera, then Provincial of Mexico, sent five Franciscan friars, who returned after two years of efforts. Their names are unknown (Cogolludo, *Historia de Yucatan*, vol. I, pp. 175, 182). The third

is the one referred to in the text.   Its commissary was Fr.
Luis de Villalpando, and its members were Fr. Lorenzo de
Bienvenida, Fr. Melchor de Benavente, Fr. Juan de Herrera,
Fr. Juan de Albalata, and Fr. Angel Maldonado.   Five other
missionaries came with Juan de la Puerta, in 1548 (Cogolludo).

22. The term *ahetzil*, I do not find, and translate it as
aheɔil, the practice of conjuring, or sorcery.   But it is quite
possibly for *ahuitzil*, dwellers in the sierra.   The next line is
corrupt, and I can only guess at the meaning.   The date, Nov.
9, 1546, is correct, and the history here given of the insur-
rection of the natives at that time is substantially the same as
is told at length by Cogolludo (*Hist. de Yucatan*, Lib. V,
cap. VII).

27. The Auditor Tomas Lopez came from Guatemala (not
Spain) to Yucatan in 1551 or 1552, and in the latter year pro-
mulgated his "Laws" for the government of the natives,
many of which are given in Cogolludo's History.

The passing reference to the cruelties of the Spaniards are
more than borne out by the testimony of Fr. Lorenzo de Bienvenida.   Writing to the King in 1548 he says :—

" En esta villa (Valladolid) se levantaron este año de qua-
renta y siete los Indios * * * i este levantamiento por mal
tratamiento que hacen à los Indios los Españoles tomandoles
las mugeres y hijos y dandoles de palos i quebrandoles las
piernas i brazos i matandolos i desmasiados tributos i desafor-
ados servicios personales, i si Vª Altª no provee de remedio
con brevedad, no es possible permanecer esta tierra, digo de
justicia. * * * *

"(El adelantado) dió la capitania à un sobrino que llaman
Manso Pacheco.   Nero no fué mas cruel que este.   Este pasó
adelante y llegó á una provincia que llaman *Chatemal*, estan-

do de paz, i sin dar guerra los naturales la robó i les comió
los mantenimientos à los naturales, i ellos huyendo à los
montes de miedo de los Españoles porque en tomando algu-
no luego lo aperreaban, i desto huian los Indios i no sembra-
ban i todos murieron de hambre, digo todos porque habia
pueblos de á quinientos casas i de á mil, i el que agora tiene
ciento es mucho ; provincia rica de cacao.   Este capitan por
sus proprias manos exercitaba las fuerzas, con un garrote maté
muchos i decia, ' este es buen palo para castigar á estos ;' i
desque lo habia muerto, 'O, quan bien lo dé.'   Corto muchos
pechos á mugeres, i manos á hombres i narices i orejas i esta-
co, i á las mugeres ataba calabazas á los pies i las echaba
en las lagunas ahogar por su pasatiempo, i otras grandes cruel-
dades." *Carta de Fr. Lorenzo de Bienvanida,* 1548. *MS.*

28. The town Conah Itza, or Con Ahitza, Con of the
Itzas, may refer to the seaport, Coni, the eastern coast, where
Montejo landed on his first expedition. Bishop Toral did not
arrive in Yucatan until 1562, so the mention of him proves
that this narrative was written after that date.

29. No such person as Juan de Montejo is known.

30. *Yocol peten ;* so it is first spelled in the original manuscript, and afterwards altered to *Yucalpeten.*   This latter
occurs as a name applied to the peninsula, or a portion of it,
in a number of passages of the Book of Chilan Balam of Chumayel.   These have been quoted by the Canon Crescencio
Carrillo in a recent work (*Historia Antigua de Yucatan,* pp.
137, 140, Merida, 1882), to support his view that the name
Yucatan is an abbreviation of Yucalpeten.

Apart from the difficulty of explaining such an extensive
abbreviation, which is not at all in the spirit of the Maya
tongue, the words of Pech in this section and § 33 conclusively

prove that the two names are entirely distinct in origin. Carrillo is of opinion that *yucal* should be divided into *y*, *u*, *cal*, and he translates the name "la perla de la garganta de la tierra ó continente." This appears far-fetched. *Yocal* is probably merely *yoc hail*, upon the water (*il*, determinative ending denoting what water); hence *yocal peten*, the region upon the water, applied to Yucatan or some part of its coast district. The *h* is nearly mute and frequently elided, as in *ocola* (*ocol haa*) to baptize.

A prophecy of the priest Pech, which is perhaps the one here referred to, appears in several of the Books of Chilan Balam, and also Spanish translations of it in the Histories of Lizana and Cogolludo, and a French version in Brasseur's report of the *Mission Scientifique au Mexique*, etc.

The text is quite corrupt, but I insert it as I have emended it from a comparison of three copies.

U Than Ahau Pech Ahkin.

Tu kinil uil u natabal kine,
Yume ti yokcab te ahtepal.
Uale canɔit u katunil,
Uchi uale hahal pul.
Tu kin kue yoklal u kaba,
In kubene yume.
Ti a-uich-ex tu bel a uliah, Ahitza,
U yum cab ca ulom.
Than tu chun ahau Pech ahkin,
Tu kinil uil can ahau katun,
Uale tan hiɔil u katunil.

THE WORD OF THE LORD PECH, THE PRIEST.

At that time it will be well to know the tidings,
Of the Lord, the ruler of the world.
After four katuns,
Then will occur the bringing of the truth.
At that time one who is a god by his name,
I deliver to you as a lord.
Be your eyes on the road for your guest, Men of Itza,
When the lord of the earth shall come.
The word of the first lord, Pech, the priest,
At the time of the fourth katun,
At the end of the katun.

The only line in which I have taken much liberty with the text is the fifth, where, after the word *kue,* one MS. reads : *yok taa ba akauba,* and another, *yok lac kauba,* neither of which is intelligible.

If the date assigned in these lines be a correct one, they were delivered by the prophet in 1469. It is not impossible. The words are obscure and the prediction so indistinct that it might quite well have been made by an official augur at that time.

31. Nachi Cocom, head of the ancient and powerful Cocom family, ruled at Zotuta when Montejo made his settlement at Merida, and was a determined enemy of the Spaniards. He was defeated in 1542, in a sanguinary battle, and then accepted terms of peace. I have in my possession the copy of a survey which he made of the lands of the town of Zotuta in 1545, when he was evidently on good terms with the Conquerors.

32. The names Chan, Catzim and Chul belong to well

known ancient Yucatecan families, and many who bear them are still found among the natives (Berendt, *Nombres Proprios en Lengua Maya*, MS.)

The words Zacuholpatal Zacmutixtun are rendered by Avila as proper names, and I have followed his example. I have not found a satisfactory explanation of them.

33. The day *One Imix* was a day of peculiar sanctity in ancient Yucatan. Landa makes the rather unintelligible assertion that the count of their days, or their calendar, invariably commenced on that day (*Relacion*, p. 236).

Imix is the 18th day of the month, and it is possibly that it and the two following days were used for intercalary days.

More to the purpose of explaining the prophecy in the text is the statement of Francisco Hernandez, who, as reported by Bishop Las Casas, relates that in the mythology of the Mayas, the god or gods Bacab, those who support the four corners of the heaven and who are identified with the "year bearers" or Dominical days of the calendar, died on the day One Imix, and after three days came to life again. (Las Casas, *Historia Apologetica de las Indias Occidentales*, cap. CXXIII.) This has reference apparently to the intercalary days Imix, Ik, and Akbal, which were counted so as to allow the next Kin Katun period to begin on I Kan. I have explained this theory fully in a paper, "Notes on the Codex Troano and Maya Chronology," in the *American Naturalist*, Sept. 1881. Naturally this was supposed by the Spanish missionaries to be a reference to Christian traditions.

Ca tip u chemob, when the ships were rocking; *tipil* represents the slipping and sliding movement of a partially submerged or hidden body; thus the beating of the heart and the pulse is *tipilac*. *Ca yumtah banderas ob*, when the banners waved ; *yumtah* is to swing to and fro as a hamack or a flag. *Piixtahob*, from *pixitah*, to unreel or reel off yarn, etc., from a spindle.   I suppose it refers to letting go the anchor.

The derivation of the name Yucatan here given is interesting, for several reasons.   In the first place, it makes it evident that Pech did not believe it was an abbreviation of Yucalpeten (see ante, page 255).   Again, although it has very often been stated that the name arose from a misunderstanding of some native words by the Spaniards, there has been no uniformity of opinion as to what these words were.   Several of the phrases suggested have been such as have no meaning in the Maya tongue ; (see full discussions of the question in Eligio Ancona, *Historia de Yucatan*, Vol. I, pp. 219, 220, and Crescencio Carrillo, *Historia Antigua de Yucatan*, cap. V.)   As given by Pech it is perfectly intelligible and good Maya.   Without syncope it would be " *Matan ca ubah a than* " shortened to " *Ma c'ubah than*, " We do not understand your speech."   Pech is in error, however, in supposing that the name arose on the arrival of Montejo ; it was in use immediately after the expedition of Cordova (1517), and if Bernal Diaz was correct in his recollection, was applied to the land by the Indians Cordova brought back to Cuba with him from the Bay of Campeachy. (See Bernal Diaz, *Historia Verdadera de la Conquista de Nueva España*, cap. VII.)

34. This is no doubt the same occurrence which is described at considerable length by Cogolludo, *Hist. de Yucatan*, Lib. III, cap. VI.   But the details differ very much and the names of the messengers and the chief to whom they were sent are not identical.   I believe this discrepancy can be explained, but it would extend this note too far to go into the subject here.   The word *yacatunzabin*, which Avila renders " en

dicha cueva," seems a compound of *y, actun, zabin.* The last is the name of the weasel; *actun* means both a cave and a stone house. By some it is supposed to be a compound of *ac*, tortoise, and *tun*, stone, a cave resembling a hollow tortoise shell.

35. *Yoklal maix u lukul yol nacomob,* "porque no se cansaban los capitanes" (Avila).

36. Pech adds a list of the names of Conquistadores which I have not inserted, as it is less complete than that found in Cogolludo.

39. *Ma u manbal cuntahbalob u chinal;* Avila translates this "that they shall not destroy"; but the word *cuntahbal*, from *cun, cumtah,* means that which is to be enchanted, and *chinal* is the throwing of stones. I suppose, therefore, it refers to some act of shamanism the design of which was to injure a neighbor.

VOCABULARY.

Ac, n. A turtle ; a turtle shell.

Actun, n. (From *ac*, turtle shell, *tun*, stone.) A cave ; a stone house.

Ah, A prefix signifying possession or action ; also sign of masculine. See pp. 28, 57.

Ahau, n. (From *ah*, prefix, and *u*, collar? See p. 57.) A ruler, chief, king ; a period of time.

Ahbalcab, n. The coming dawn. "Quiere amanescer." *Dicc. Motul.*

Ahez, n. (From *ah*, prefix, *ezah*, to show, to feign.) A sorcerer, magician.

Ahkin, n. (From *ah*, and *kin*, the sun, day, etc.) A priest.

Ahkulel, n. (From *ah* and *kulel*, to arrange business, etc.) A lieutenant, deputy. pp. 27, 247.

Ahoni, n. Well-dressed persons. p. 173.

Ahpul, n One who carries or bears.

Ahpulul, n. He or that which is carried or brought.

Ahtepal, n. A ruler, governor.

Ahtohil, n. A lover of justice ; a righteous man.

Ahuitzil, n. Mountaineers. p. 131.

Ak, n. Osiers, willow branches. "Ramo de miembre." Pio Perez. *Dicc.*

Akab, n. Night, the night time.

Al, n. Son or daughter of a woman. *Yal*, her son.

Alah, v. pres. *alic*, fut. *alab*. To speak, say, tell, order.

Alau, A numeral. p. 46.

Anahte. n. A book. p. 64.

Atan, n. Wife.

Auat, v. aor. *autah*, fut. *auté*. To shout, to sing. "Dar gritos."

261

Cal, n. Throat, neck; voice; in compos. an intensive particle.

Calab, A numeral. p. 45.

Cambezah, v. To teach, to instruct.

Can, n. 1. Conversation, talk. 2. The generic name for serpents. 3. The number four. 4. A gift or present.

Can, v. aor. *tah*, fut. *té*. To converse, to tell stories. aor. *ah*, fut. *é*. To teach, to impart information; to give another a contagious disease.

Can, part. in compos. Strongly, powerfully, as *cankax*, to tie very firmly.

Canantah, v. To watch, to guard over.

Canlaahal, v. To learn about.

Caputzihil, n. Baptism (*ca*, twice, *zihil*, to be born; an ancient word; see Landa, *Relacion*, p. 144).

Catac, conj. And; used to connect numerals. p. 49.

Caten, adv. The second time. *Tu caten*, for the second time. (From *ca*, *two*.)

Catul, adv. Two. *Tu catulli*, both, the two.

Caua, conj. And, then.

Cax, n. A fowl, a hen.

Caxan, v, aor. *tah*, fut. *té*. To seek, to find, to hunt for.

Caxtun, adv. Then, be it so, thus.

Ceh, n. A deer.

Cen, v. irreg. aor. *cihi*, fut. *ciac*. To say, to tell.

Ci, Cici, part. These prefixes mean pleasant, agreeable; originally, what is pleasant to taste.

Cibah, v. aor. *cibhi*, fut. *cibic*. To wish, to permit, to dare. *U cibah ua a yum.* Did your father permit it?

Cicithan, n. (From *cici*, pleasant, *than*, words.) Words of love or blessing.

Ciciol, n. (From *cici* and *ol*.) Joy, pleasure, peace, happiness.

Cii, n. The pulque liquor. See p. 22.

Cill, n. Delight, pleasure.

Cilich, adj. Saintly, holy.

Cob, v. 3d pl. pres. indic. of *cen*.

Cimil, v. To die.

Coch, in comp. Conveys the notion of extending or broadening.

Cochhal *or* Cochlahal, v. To make broad, to extend, to spread out.

Cuch, n. 1. Position, place. 2. Burden, load; *met.* sin. 3. Goods, possessions, treasures.

Cuch, v. aor. *ah*, fut. *é.* 1. To carry, to bear along. 2. To govern a town or state.

Cuchcabal, n. A province, region; the family, people or subjects of one ruler.

Cuchhab, n. The year-bearer or Dominical sign. p. 52.

Cuchi. Sign of past tense. p. 29.

Cuchul, n. The family or retainers of one person. "La familia ó gente que uno tiene en su casa." *Dicc. Motul.*

Cul, n. A vase or cup.

Culcinah, v. To appoint, to promote, to establish; *culcinta-haan,* appointed or promoted to an office or dignity.

Cultal *or* Cutal, v. aor. *culhi*, fut. *culac.* To sit down, remain, be present, be at home, etc.

Culul *or* Cuulul *or* Culicil, v. To rest or stop; to reside, to settle down.

Cum *or* Cuum, n. A vase, jar.

Cumcintah, v. To prepare for use, to put in order. Probably a form of *culcinah.*

Cumlaahaal, v. To stop, to check.

Cumtal, v. aor. *lahi*, fut. *ac.* To set up, to put in a place.

Cun *or* Cunah *or* Cunal, n. Enchantment, sorcery, conjury. *Au ohel ua* u *cunal chuplal?* Do you know the conjury of a woman? *Dicc. Motul (i. e.,* to make her submit to the will of a man).

Cuntabal, Passive supine; from *cunah,* to conjure.

Cutz, n. The wild turkey,

Ch.

Chac, n. Water, rain, a giant, a god. adj. red. In comp. much or very.

Chacaan, n. Something plain, open, visible.

Chacanhal, v. To become visible, to show itself.

Chahal, v. To lose strength, to weaken.

Chakan, n. A savanna. p. 125.

Chapahal, v. To sicken.

Chayanil, n. The rest, the remainder.

Che, n. A tree; wood; *adj.* wooden.

Chem, n. A boat, a ship.

Chen, adv. Solely, only, merely.

Chenbel, adv. Vainly, fruitlessly.

Chi, n. The mouth; a border, limit, edge; a bite, as *u chi pek*, the bite of a dog.
verb, to bite, to eat.

Chicilbezah, v. To set landmarks, to point out.

Chichcunah, v. To strengthen, to fortify.

Chichcunahthan, v. To support another's words, to agree with, to act in concert with. p. 107.

Chicul, n. A sign, mark, token.

Chikin, n. The West.

Chicpahal, v. aor. *pahi*, fut. *pahac*. To find, to discover, to recover that which is lost; "parecerlo perdido." Pio Perez, *Dicc.*

Chilan, n. An interpreter. p. 69.

Chin, v. aor. *ah*, fut. *è*. To stone, to throw stones at.

Chin, adj. A term of endearment.

Chinchin, v. To incline, lean over, be out of line.

Choy, n. A bucket; *choyche*, a wooden bucket.

Chuuc *or* Chuc, v. aor. *ah*, fut. *è*. To grasp, seize, to take possession of.

Chucan, n. Completeness, sufficiency, abundance.

Chuccabil, n. A province, district.

Chul, n. A flute.

Chulub, n. Rain water; reservoirs.

Chun, n. Foundation; trunk (of a tree); beginning; cause.

R

Chunbezah, v.　To cause, to occasion, to begin.

Chunthan, n.　(From *chun*, first, *than*; speech, he who speaks first.)　A principal, a presiding officer.

Cħ

Cħaa, *or* **Cħaab,** v.　aor. *cħaah*, fut. *chaé*.　1. To take, to carry; to carry off; hence to kill.　2. To recover that which is lost.

Cħahucil or Cħuhucil, n.　Sweets.

Cħeen, n.　Lowland; well.　pp. 33, 125.

Cħibal, n.　Lineage, generation.

Cħuplal, n.　Woman, girl.

Cħuytab, v.　To hang.

E

Et, A particle indicating similitude.　As a verb, to hold alike in the two hands.　Hence, *eta*, friend; *etel*, companion; *etan*, wife; *etcah*, fellow townsman; *yetel*, and, with, etc.

Ez, n.　Enchanter, sorcerer.

Ezah, v.　To show, to make public; to imitate, feign.　*Ezabil*, what is to be or should be shown or published.

H

Haa, n.　Water.

Haab, n.　Year.　p. 50.

Haban, n.　Branch, twig.　p. 126.

Hach, adv.　Much, very.

Hahal, adj. and adv.　True, truly.

Halach, adj. and n.　True, truth; *halach than*, an oath; *halach uinic.*　p. 26.

Halal, n.　The cane.

Hanal, v.　aor. *hani*, fut. *hanac*.　To eat.

Haual, v.　aor. *haui*, fut. *hauac*.　To cease, to stop.

Hayal, v.　To level with the ground, to destroy; from *hay*, thin, flat; hence *hayalcab*, the final end and destruction of the world.

Heɔ *or* Eɔ, v. aor. *ah*, fut. *é*. To fix firmly, to establish, to found; to select a site.

Heɔcab, v. To fix or establish promptly; "poner ó afirmar ó asentar de presto alguna cosa que quede ferme." *Dicc. Motul.*

Hicħcal, v. To tie up by the neck, to hang.

Hiɔ *or* Hiɔil, n. The close or last of the week, month, or year, as *u hiɔil buluc ahau katun*, the last day of the eleventh Ahau katun. *Chilan Balam.*

Ho, adj. Five.

Hokol, v. aor. *hoki*. To set out for, to go out from; of seeds, to sprout; of the beard, etc., to begin to grow.

Hokzahuba, v. To take oneself away from.

Hol, n. The end of anything, hence the door of a house, the gate of a town, the mouth of a bag or jar, a hole, an aperture; verb, sensu obscœno, to seduce a girl, to penetrate her. *Dicc. Motul.*

Holcan, n. A warrior; adj. brave, valiant.

Holhaa, n. A seaport. See *haa.*

Holpay, n. A seaport. See *pay.*

Holpop, n. A chieftain (from *hol* and *pop*, mat); "he who is at the end or head of the mat."

Hom, n. A trumpet.

Hoppol, v. To begin.

Hun, adj. One.

Hunakbu, n. The one God.

Hunkul, adv. Once and forever, really, permanently.

Hunmol, adj. United together, congregated in one place

Hunten, adv. On one occasion, at one time.

Huun, n. A book. p. 63.

I.

Ich, n. 1. Face; eyes; twins; surface. 2. Fruit; longing; color.

Ich, prep. In, into, within.

Ilah, v. aor. *ilah*, fut. *ilé*. or *ilab*. To see, to look at, to visit, to test, to try.

Ix, fem. prefix. See page 28; conj. and also n. urine.

Ixim, n. Maize.

Ixmehen, n. A daughter.

K.

Kaan, n. A measure. p. 27.

Kab, n. The hand, the arm.

Kaba, n. A name. See p. 26.

Kabanzah, v. To give a name.

Kah, n. Pinole, meal of roasted maize, used for stirring in water to drink.

Kahal, v. To remember, recall.

Kahlay, n. Memory, memorial, record.

Kak, n. Fire; also a febrile disease.

Kaknab, n. The sea, the ocean.

Kal, n. A score. p. 39; verb, to imprison.

Kam *or* **Kamah**, v. To accept, receive; to take possession of.

Kan, adj. Yellow. n. The name of the first day of the Maya month.

Kat, v. To wish, to desire. To ask, to ask for, to inquire.

Katun, n. A body of warriors; a period of time. p. 58.

Kax, n. Forest, woods.

Kaxah, v. To join, unite, tie together.

Kay *or* **Kayah**, v. To sing.

Keban, n. Sin, evil.

Kebanthan, v. To plot evil, to calumniate; to commit treason; " kebanthanil, traicion." *Dicc. Motul.*

Kilacale, n. Ancestors.

Kin, n. The sun; a day; time.

Kinchil. A numeral. p. 46.

Koch *or* **Kooch**, v. To carry on the shoulders as a burden, hence, *fig.* n. obligation, fault, sickness.

Kohan, n. Sickness.

Ku, n. God, divinity.

Kubulte, n. Delivery, deposit.

Kuchul, v. aor. *kuchi*, fut. *kuchuc*. To arrive, to come to.

Kul, in comp. much, very; *kulvinic*. pp. 133, 164.

Kuna, n. (From *ku*, god, *na*, house). A temple, a church.

Kuuch, n. Cotton threads.

Kuxil, n. Aversion, disgust, annoyance; verb. to feel disgust at.

Kuyan, adj. Consecrated to God, holy.

L

Lahal, v. To finish, to end.

Lahca. Twelve.

Lahun. Ten. p. 38.

Lai *or* Lay, rel. and dem. pron. This, that, these, those, which, what, etc.

Lak, n. Companion, neighbor.

Lic *or* Licil, rel. In which, by which.

Likil, v. To rise, to raise; as *likil katun*, to begin war.

Likin *or* Lakin, n. The East.

Likul, prep. From, out of.

Likzah, v. To lift up, to raise; *likzahuba*, to raise oneself.

Loh, v. To redeem, to set at liberty.

Lohil, n. The Redeemer, the Saviour.

Lukanil, n. That which is set apart or separated.

Lukul, v. aor. *luki*, fut. *lukuc*. To leave a place, to depart from, go out of.

Lukzah, v. To free, to separate from; *lukzahuba*, to quit, to abstain from.

M

Ma, adv. No, not. From this are the negatives, *matan*, not, emphatic; *mato, matac, maina*, not even; *maix, matla*, neither; *mamac*, no one; *manan*, without, etc.

Mac, rel. pron. Who.

Maccah, v. To obstruct, close up roads, etc. Hence *macan* p. p. p. that which is obstructed.

Mach, v. aor. *ah*, fut. *è*. To take with the hand, to hold in the hand.

Mactzil, adj. Marvelous, miraculous; n. a miracle, an act of Providence. (From *mac*, most, and *tzibil*, to be obeyed or reverenced.)

Mak, v. To eat soft things, to eat without chewing.

Mal *or* **Malel,** v. aor. *mani*, fut. *manac*. To pass.

Manak, n. A sign or mark.

Manal, adv. Too much, in excess.

Manbal, adv. Nothing.

Mat, v. To receive, obtain.

Maya, n. Derivation of. p. 16.

Mayacimil, n. The pestilence. p. 132.

Mazcab, n. A prison, gaol.

Mazeual, n. Vassal, servant. Nahuatl, *maceualli*.

Mehen, n. A son.

Mek, n. An armful, hence

Mektantah, *or* **Mektanma,** v. To hold in one's power, to rule, govern.

Mektancah, n. Jurisdiction, municipality.

Mektanmail, n. A ruler, governor.

Mentah, v. To make, manufacture.

Menyah, v. To work, serve. n. Work, service.

Met, n. A wheel. p. 86.

Mex *or* **Meex,** n. The beard.

Meyah, v. To serve, to labor for one.

Minantal, v. p. p. minaan. To lack, to be absent or wanting, not to have.

Molcintah, v. To gather together, join, unite.

Moltah, v. To gather around.

Mothtal, v. To humble, to submit.

Muk, n. Fortitude, bravery.

Muktan, v. To suffer with fortitude.

Mul *or* Mol, part. in comp. Jointly, in common.

Mulba, v. To congregate, to come together.

Multepal, v. To rule or govern jointly. p. 131.

Muz, v. To cut.

N

Na, n. A house, not designating whose.

Naat, v. To know, understand.

Nacal, v. To ascend. p. 28.

Nachi, adv. Far off, distant.

Nacpalancal, v. To grope, to feel one's way.

Nah, v. To suit, wish, desire; *nahuba*, to suit, etc., for oneself.

Nak, n. The abdomen, belly, the end; verb. to end, finish; to join, to stick; *tu nak*, at the end, near, close to.

Nakal, v. To approach, to join on.

Nant, v. See *Naat*.

Noh, adj. Great, large.

Nohkakil, n. Smallpox. p. 132.

Nohoch, adj. Great, large.

Nohol, n. The South.

Nuc, adj. Great, large.

Nuc, v. To answer; n. an answer.

Nuctah, v. To understand, perceive.

Nucté, adj. Old, ancient; *nucteel*, the elders and leading men of a town.

Nucul, n. Signification, meaning; manner, form, figure.

Numya, n. Toil, misery, unhappiness.

Nucahthan, v. To reply, to answer.

Nupthan, n. Companion, associate.

O

Oc, n. The foot; *yooc* his foot, their feet.

Oca *or* Ochaa *or* Ocolha, (From v. *ocol*, to enter, *haa*, water,) To baptize.

Ocnakuchil, n. A pestilence. p. 151.

Ocol, v. aor. *oci*, fut. *ococ*. To enter; also *sensu obscœno.*

Ohel, v. aor. *tah*, fut. *té.* To know, to recognize.

Ol, n. Mind, intention, will.

Olah, v. To wish, to desire; n. will, good will, wish.

On, pron. We.

Ontkin, adv. For a long time.

Op *or* Oop, n. The anona, custard apple.

Otoch, n. House, dwelling, denoting whose. p. 106.

Ox, adv. Three; *oxlahun*, thirteen. p. 130.

P

Pa *or* Paa, n. A walled town, stronghold, fortress. p. 163.

Pa, v. To break, break down, destroy.

Pach, To take possession of, to select a place.

Pach, n. The back of the shoulders; the outer or back part; hence, the last or end of anything; *tu pach*, behind, after.

Pachal, adv. Afterwards, late.

Paiche, n. A mark, a line.

Pak *or* Pakil, n. A wall of stone. verb, aor. *ah*, fut. *é.* To found, build, sow, plant; hence

Pakal, n. A building, founding, etc.

Pakte *or* Pakteil, adv. All together, in all.

Palil, n. A servant, man-servant.

Pan, n. Standard, banner.

Patan, n. Tribute, tax; from *paatah*, to watch, to guard.

Patcunah, v. To declare, set forth, explain; n. an explanation, etc.

Paxal *or* Paaxal, v. aor. *xi*, fut. *xac*. To forsake, abandon, desert, depopulate; "desamparar y despoblar pueblo." *Dicc. Motul.*

Pay, n. The sea-coast.

Pay, v. aor. *tah*, fut. *té*. To draw or call toward one, hence, *payal*, to be called or summoned.

Paybe, n. (From *pay*, and *be*, a road). A guide; hence, adv., first, before.

Pek, n. A dog.

Pet, n. A circle, wheel.

Peten, n. An island, country, province. p. 122.

Pic. A numeral. p. 45.

Pix *or* Piixtah, v. To unwind, to cast anchor.

Pixan, n. Soul; happiness; adj. happy.

Pol. n. Head; hair.

Puchtun, n. Fighting, quarreling.

Puczical, n. Heart; mind, will, soul.

Pul, v. To bring, to carry. *Ahpulul*, one who brings.

Pp

Ppatal, v. To remain, to stay.

Ppiz, n. A measure of grain, etc.

Ppoc, n. A hat.

Ppul *or* Ppuul, n. An earthen jar.

T

Taab, n. Salt.

Tab, v. To tie together; hence

Tabal, n. Relationship; anything attached to or dependent on another.

Tabzah, v.　To deceive, to delude, to tie.

Tah, adv.　Whence, whither, thence, to, unto. pron.　For us, for our part.

Takal, v.　To stick to; to add to, to increase.

Tal, prep.　From; *tii tal en,* I am from there. *Dicc. San Francisco.*

Tal, v. aor. *ah,* fut. *é.*　To touch, to begin to take; to make use of.

Talel, v. aor. *tali,* fut. *talae* or *tae.*　To come, to go.

Tamuk, adv.　While, when.

Tan, n.　The breast; hence, the middle of anything, as *tan cah,* the middle of the town.　p. 132.

Tan, postposition.　Toward, as *lakintan,* toward the East.

Tancabal, n.　The premises of a house; a house and its grounds.

Tancoch, n.　A half (from *tan,* and *cochil,* the width, the size of a thing).

Tec, adv.　Quickly, suddenly.

Tem *or* **Temah,** v.　To satisfy, please.

Ten, pron.　I.　*Ten c en,* I who am I.

Tepal, v.　To rule, govern.

Than, n.　Word, speech.

Thun, n.　A drop, a spot, a dot.

Ti, prep. To, by, for; sign of dative and ablative.　‘

Tiihil, v. To happen there, to take place there.

Tipp, v. To exceed in size; to go forth from; as *tippan kin,* the sun having appeared.

Toc *or* **Tooc,** v. aor. *tocah,* fut. *é,*　To burn.

Toch, adj. Severe, firm, rough.

Tocoyna, n. A deserted house or field; "solar yermo." *Dicc. Motul.*

Toh, adj. Just, righteous; *ahtohil,* a magistrate.

Tohyol, adj. Healthy, well (from *toh, ol*).

Tox, v. To pour out; *tox haa ti pol,* to pour water on the head, *i. e.,* to baptize. *Dicc. Motul. Toxol,* the person baptized; also a distribution or outpouring, as *toxol cahob,* a distribution of towns to different rulers.

Tul, adj. Full, abounding. p. 39.
verb. To fill to overflowing, to rise (of the tide). For *tutul* see p. 109.

Tulpach, v. To go back, to return.

Tulum, n. A wall, walled town. p. 163.

Tumen, prep. For, by reason of, because of.

Tun, n. A stone. A euphonic particle. p. 124.

Tux *or* **Tuux,** adv. Where, in what part or place.

Tuzebal, adv. Promptly.

Tuzinil, adv. All, in all parts.

Tzac, v. To seek, to follow.

Tzen, n. Food, sustenance; hence,

Tzentah, To give food to.

Tzicil, v. To obey, to serve.

Tzimin, n. A horse.

Tzol, n. A string, thread; hence, verb, to arrange on a string, to put in order, to adjust; *tzolan,* an arrangement, series, order.

Tzuc, n. A part, division. p. 54.

Tzucub, n. A province.

U

U, n. The moon; a month; menstrual period; a string of beads, a collar; rosary. pron. His, her, its, their. Also a euphonic particle before vowels.

Uaatal, v. To set up, erect.

Uabic, adv. How, in what manner.

Uac, Six.

Uacchahal, v. To emerge with force. p. 185.

Uacuntah, v. To set on end, to put in place; to designate, appoint; *uacuntahbal*, the putting in place, etc.

Uah, n. Tortilla, bread; *uahal uahob.* p. 129.

Uahil, n. Banquet; guest.

Ualac, adv. While, meanwhile.

Ualkahal, v. To turn oneself, to return.

Uaxac, Eight.

Uay *or* **Uai,** adv. Here, in this place.

Uazaklom, n. A return. p. 86.

Ubah, v. To hear, understand.

Uchebal, conj. In order that.

Uchul, v. aor. *uchi*, fut. *uchuc.* To happen, to occur, take place, come to pass.

Uinalal, n. Labor, work.

Uinbail, n. Image, figure.

Uinic, n. Man; a measure. p. 27.

Uitz, n. A mountain, a hill. p. 131.

Ulul, v. To arrive, return.

Ulum, n. A bird, a pheasant.

Uooh, v. To write. p. 63.

Utial, prep. For, on account of.

Utz, adj. Good; *utzil*, the good, the well-being.

Utzcinah, v. To make better, to perfect; to compose a speech or essay; to set in order.

Utzuac, adv. Now, be it now.

Uuc. Seven.

Uuɔ, n. A folding, doubling; a line of warriors.

X

Xachetah, v. To seek, to procure.

Xamach, n. A large pot or jar.

Xaman, n. The North.

Xan, n. Straw ; conj. also adv. slowly.

Xantal, v. aor. *xanhi* fut. *xanac*. To stay behind, to remain.

Xenhi, v. To vomit.

Xic, v. To split, to divide.

Xicin, n. The ear, the hearing.

Ximbal, v. to journey, to pass.

Xiu, n. Grass, herbage, name of a noble family. p. 109.

Xma, prep. Without.

Xocol, v. To count, to read.

Xotlahal, v. To cut.

Xul, n. End, limit ; v. to end,. also *xulul*.

Y

Ya, n. 1. Love. 2. Pain, wound, sickness. 3. Difficulty. 4. A shoe.

Yaab, adj. Much, abundant : *yaabil*, abundance, multitude.

Yacunah, v. To love.

Yah *or* Yaah, n. Severe sickness.

Yala, The rest, remainder.

Yalan, prep. Under, beneath.

Yan *or* Yanhal, v. To have, to be, to stand.

Yax, adv. First, freshly ; adj. green, young.

Yaxchun, n. The beginning, cause.

Yetel, conj. And, with, a compound of *u etel*, his or its companion, usually abbreviated *to y*.

Yib, n. A bean.

Yic, n. Red peppers.

Yok, prep. On, over, in front of.

Yoklal, prep. By reason of, because of.

Yokolcab, adv. On the earth, in the world.

Yol, n. Mind, spirit.

Yxma, prep. Without, = *xma*.

Yub, n. Cloak, coat.

Yum, n. Father; lord; ruler; head of a family.

Yum *or* Yumtah, v. To wave, to move to and fro.

Z

Zabin, n. A weasel.

Zah *or* Zahal *or* Zahacil, n. Fear, terror; verb, to fear.

Zat, v. aor. *ah*, fut. *é*. To lose.

Zi, n. Wood.

Zihnal, n. Birth, a native.

Zil *or* Ziil, v. To give, to present; n. gifts.

Zinah, v. To cut wood.

Zuhuy, n. A virgin.

Zulbil-taab, n. Purified salt, from *zul*, to soak.

Zut, v. To return; *tu zut pach*, back again, over again.

Ɔ

Ɔa v. aor. *ɔaah*, fut. *ɔaé* or *ɔaab*. To give; *ɔabal*, past part. pas. that which is to be given.

Ɔa, v. To avail, to be of advantage.

Ɔaleb, n. A seal, mould, press.

Ɔan, v. To devastate, ruin.

Ɔaɔ, v. To suck; *ɔaɔopob*, suckers of anonas, a name given to the Spaniards.

Ɔiboltah, v. To desire, wish for.

Ɔib *or* Ɔibah, v. To write.

Ɔicil, n. Bravery; encouragement.

Ɔilibal, n. A register, record.

Ɔoc, n. The end, the last.
  v. To happen, to occur; to tear down.
  adv. Already.

Ɔoocol, v. To end, finish.

Ɔuɔ, v. To kiss, to suck.

Ɔuunɔucil, adj. Made of mud, or plastered.

Ɔul, n. A foreigner, stranger. p. 131.

Ɔunul, v. To make a beginning.

Ɔuɔucinzah, v. To act mildly and kindly; from ɔuɔ, to kiss, to suck.

www.ingramcontent.com/pod-product-compliance
Lightning Source LLC
Chambersburg PA
CBHW030730280326
41926CB00086B/977